PAY DIRT!

The Search for Gold in British Columbia

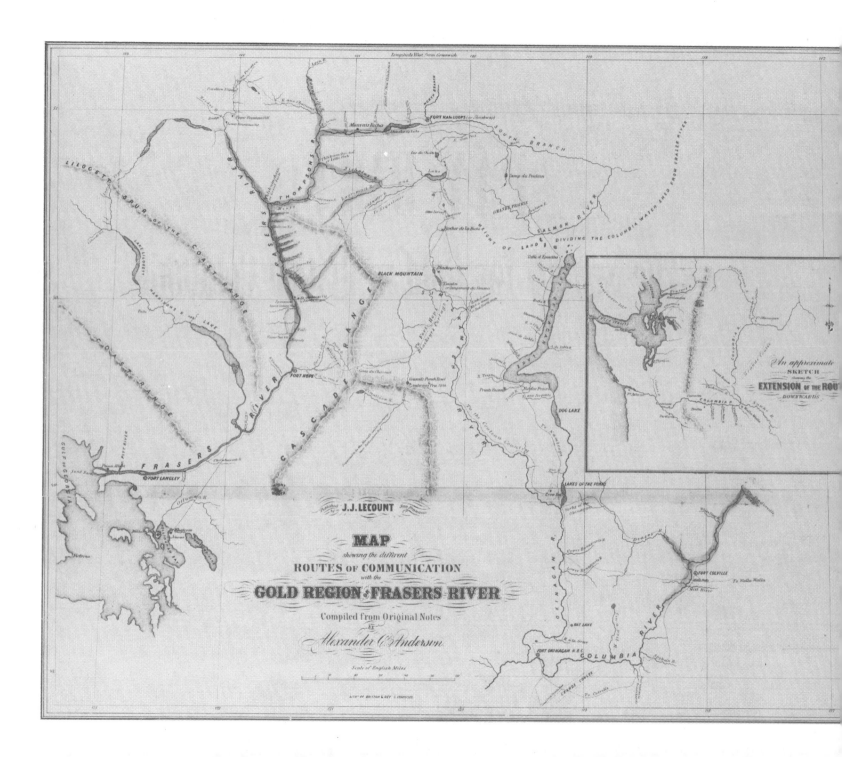

An approximate
SKETCH
shewing the
EXTENSION OF THE ROUTE
DOWNWARDS

Published by
J. J. LECOUNT San Francisco

MAP
shewing the different
ROUTES OF COMMUNICATION
with the
GOLD REGION on FRASERS RIVER

Compiled from Original Notes
by
Alexander C. Anderson

Scale of English Miles

LITH. OF BRITTON & REY S. FRANCISCO

PAY DIRT!

The Search for Gold in British Columbia

Written by
LAURA LANGSTON

Illustrated by
STUART DUNCAN

ORCA BOOK PUBLISHERS

Thanks to Ann Featherstone for the phone call that started everything rolling. Thanks also to Sandi Grove-White for enthusiastically supplying me with valuable books and information very early on; to the staff at the Provincial Archives in Victoria, in particular Kelly Nolan and Brian Young, for their patience in answering questions and dealing with requests; to librarian Sharon Ferris at the Ministry of Energy, Mines and Petroleum Resources for her invaluable assistance in digging out bits of information; to the chief gold commissioner of British Columbia, Denis Lieutard, for his discerning eye and welcome comments on the final manuscript; and to Christine Toller whose dedication to finding just the right picture can be seen on every page.

Finally, thanks must go to Vickie Kampe, who struggled through many challenging mornings with Zachary while I wrote and polished this book.

Canadian Cataloguing in Publication Data
Langston, Laura, 1958–
  Pay dirt!

Includes index.
ISBN 1-55143-029-0

1. British Columbia—Gold discoveries—Juvenile literature. 2. Gold mines and mining—British Columbia—Juvenile literature. I. Title.

FC3820.G6L36 1995   j971.1   C95–910214-0
F1087.4.L36 1995

Publication assistance provided by The Canada Council

Design by Christine Toller
Illustrations by Stuart Duncan

All photographs, illustrations and paintings are reproduced with the permission of the British Columbia Archives and Records Service, Victoria, BC

Printed and bound in Canada

Orca Book Publishers
PO Box 5626, Station B
Victoria, BC Canada
V8R 6S4

Orca Book Publishers
PO Box 468
Custer, WA USA
98240-0468

10 9 8 7 6 5 4 3 2 1

Table of Contents

For more than 5,000 years gold has been a symbol of everything that is good and wonderful. Consider these sayings:

"It is worth its weight in gold."

"Gold is where you find it."

"He has a heart of gold."

"She is as good as gold."

Not only do we talk about gold, but we read about it in stories and books. There are the golden apple, the golden ages, the golden gate and the golden rule, to name just a few.

Gold has fascinated men and women since the beginning of time. Ancient peoples in the Middle East made statues out of gold, while the ancient Egyptians fashioned rings and necklaces out of the gold they found in the Nile River. Gold was used to decorate clothing; golden objects were buried with the dead. Gold was even

used to bribe friends and neighbours.

The cry "gold" has lured men across rivers and oceans, over the highest mountain ranges and into burning deserts. Gold has carried civilization to many corners of the world.

And British Columbia is no exception.

This province was formed, in large part, because of a gold rush that brought thousands of men from all over the world. They came from China and Aus-
tralia; from Scotland, England and Wales; from across Canada and across the United States. They came to seek their fortunes. In the process they dug roads, built cities and established businesses. Some stayed forever. Others became discouraged and left. Most were honest, a few were not. They all sought one thing: the riches that only gold could bring. A few made fortunes. Many more didn't.

This is their story.

Chapter One

BEFORE THE RUSH BEGAN

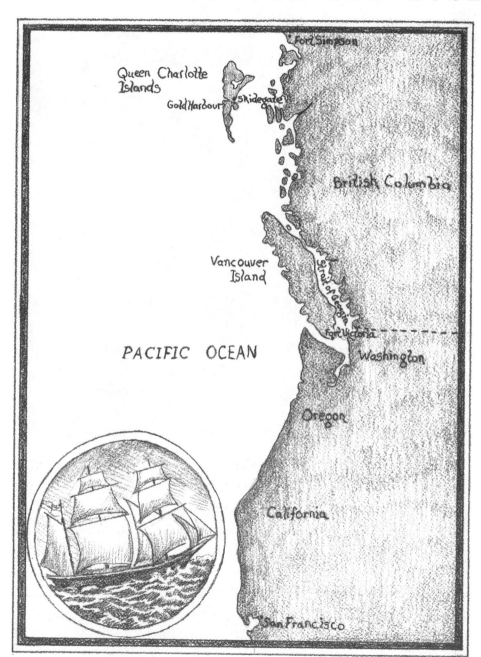

Long before the Europeans arrived, the Native people knew all about gold. But they didn't bother with it. They left it on the riverbeds and streams. It was too soft to use for weapons. They favoured iron knives and spears pointed with copper.

When the Europeans arrived, and the fur trade began in the early 1800s, the native people noticed that the Europeans valued the soft rocks he called gold. He wore it in finger rings and watch chains. As time went on, one native chief in particular realized how important gold was to the Europeans. It could be traded, he decided, for things his people needed — things like blankets and tobacco.

His English name was Albert Edenshaw, and he was a Haida chief from the Queen Charlotte Islands. He and some of his people made regular trading trips to Fort Simpson, where the Hudson's Bay Company (HBC) had its headquarters. During a trip in 1850, Edenshaw was approached by the Factor—the local boss of the HBC—who showed him an ore sample that held some gold. According to an account in Kathleen Dalzell's book *The Queen Charlotte Islands*, the Factor was very interested.

"Do you know where I can get more of this?" he asked.

Edenshaw was curious. "You want more?" he questioned.

"Yes," the Factor replied. "And I will pay well for it."

"How much?" Edenshaw asked, wondering why a rock would be so valuable.

When the Factor opened his arms in the shape of a large box and promised to fill it with enough blankets for a potlatch, Chief Edenshaw's eyes widened. Casually he promised to see what he could find.

Several weeks later, during celebrations in Skidegate, Chief Edenshaw brought out the ore and asked if anyone had more like it. One elderly woman disappeared and returned with an ore sample far better than the one in Edenshaw's hand. He asked her where she had found it and she agreed to guide him to the spot.

Early the next morning, Edenshaw, his wife, his four-year-old son and the old woman left Skidegate for Mitchell Inlet in Gold Harbour.

The adults left the child in the canoe while they climbed up the rocks to the ledge where the golden ore was found. Working carefully, Edenshaw began to chip away at the ore while his wife carefully laid it in her basket.

Finally, after many long and tiring hours, the basket was full. But Edenshaw wasn't satisfied. There were still a few hours of daylight left and he wanted to get as much gold as he could. Empty the first basket, he told his wife, and come back for more.

Albert Edenshaw

Two Kinds of Gold

There are two basic kinds of gold deposits.

There are alluvial deposits, or gold that has been washed out of original rock formations and left as dust or nuggets in creeks or gravel. This gold is often mined by panning or dredging and is sometimes called placer gold.

Vein deposits are usually found in the seams of rocks. This gold is gathered through something called lode mining or hard rock mining. And this is what Chief Edenshaw was doing. In his case, he was able to see the gold veins in the ore and chip pieces away from the larger rock. In many cases, however, the layers of gold are so thin that the rocks must be crushed and processed before any gold is found.

Dutifully, the wife emptied the first basket into the bottom of the canoe and returned to help her husband. Finally, exhausted and dirty, they were finished. They lugged the second basket to the canoe.

But most of the gold from their first basket was gone! Their little boy had grown bored. To amuse himself, he had decided to toss the pretty rocks into the ocean.

Edenshaw was furious, but there wasn't much he could do. It was almost dark and too late to chip more ore from the mountain. They returned to Skidegate, and when Edenshaw took the ore to Fort Simpson, the Factor gave him the blankets, as he'd promised.

Trading With The Europeans

When gold was first discovered on the Queen Charlottes, most of the people living there belonged to the Haida nation. The Haida were a large group—some say there were as many as 8,000 members—and they lived in coastal bays and inlets. The Haida people traded sea otter pelts with the Europeans. Trading brought them many goods they wanted, but it also brought them in contact with European diseases. The dreaded smallpox was one of those illnesses. Because so many people became ill and died, by 1915 the Haida population had fallen to just 588. In 1992 the population of the Haida peoples in B.C. was over 3,000.

Word of Edenshaw's find quickly spread. Soon other Haidas took ore samples to Fort Simpson. Realizing the gold was valuable, they began to demand high prices for it.

The Hudson's Bay Company decided to look for the ore itself. In 1851, it sent its men to Gold Harbour on a ship called the *Una*. The men tried to barter with the native people who were already at the site. But as soon as the Haidas realized the men wanted the ore, they raised the prices again. Members of the Hudson's Bay Company left, taking with them sixteen ounces of gold, worth $1,000.

Over the next year, the HBC continued to look for gold in Gold Harbour. The *Una* went back a second time. Men began blasting through the rock, looking for gold veins. When the Haida realized how much gold the men were taking, they rushed to the scene and began gathering up the flying rocks. Soon fights broke out. The Haida were determined to fight for their land. The Europeans were equally determined to get the gold. Finally the HBC left, taking about $75,000 in gold with it.

What's In A Name?

The Hudson's Bay Company at Fort Victoria.

If it weren't for Queen Victoria, the province of British Columbia might have had a completely different name.

When Chief Edenshaw discovered gold at Mitchell Inlet, the province of British Columbia hadn't even been formed yet. It was called New Caledonia and it belonged to the British. The British had gained control of the region after wrestling the area away from both the Spanish and Americans.

Most European settlers, particularly those on Vancouver Island, worked for the Hudson's Bay Company.

The HBC provided government for the settlers and controlled the fur trade. When gold was discovered, however, Britain decided to take control of New Caledonia—including Vancouver Island and the mainland—and establish a government. Many thought it made sense to keep the name New Caledonia, but in order to avoid confusion with a French colony of the same name, Queen Victoria decided to call the new region British Columbia.

But that gold, like the gold Edenshaw first found, ended up in the ocean, too. The *Una* sailed for Victoria just before Christmas in 1851. The men were anxious to get home. When the ship crashed on an uncharted reef and began to go down, the native people rushed out to gather what gold they could. Another fight ensued. A passing ship rescued the HBC crew, but as they were deserting the *Una*, an angry Native set fire to it. It sunk to the bottom of the ocean with much of its gold still intact.

Meanwhile, word of the find off the coast of New Caledonia had spread. American prospectors decided to head north and try their luck near the Queen Charlotte Islands. As soon as they arrived and saw the HBC at work, they spread in all directions looking for new gold sites.

The "Father of British Columbia"

Sir James Douglas

Often called the "Father of British Columbia," Sir James Douglas was born in British Guiana and educated in Scotland. At close to six feet and almost 250 pounds, Douglas was an imposing man who, with his military background, resembled a typical British statesman. Slightly stiff, formal and reserved, he was also honest, straightforward and a good administrator, though some said he was obsessed to a fault with small details. When he worked for the Hudson's Bay Company as a younger man, his co-workers said his only fault was he became "furiously violent when aroused."

Douglas was first sent to the West Coast in 1830 by the Hudson's Bay Company. Originally posted at a fort in Washington State, Douglas was sent north in 1843 to establish the post of Fort Victoria. After Vancouver Island was proclaimed a British colony in 1850, Douglas was appointed governor. For years, he assumed the dual role of representing the Queen and administering Fort Victoria for the HBC.

By the time the gold rush began, Douglas was almost fifty-five years old. His temper, by now, was generally under control. Because of his honesty, his fairness and his real concern for New Caledonia, Douglas earned the long-lasting respect of the native people, the Europeans and the miners.

His dedication was also recognized by Queen Victoria. In 1863, twenty years after establishing the post of Fort Victoria, Douglas announced that he would retire as governor of Vancouver Island. The Queen rewarded his hard work by granting him a knighthood. In the future, James Douglas would forever be known as Sir James Douglas.

When Douglas died in Victoria on August 4, 1877, his funeral was one of the most important events ever held in the city. Businesses shut down. Public buildings were draped with black. And while the church bells tolled for the "Father of British Columbia," a mile-long funeral procession wound through the streets of the city.

Governor Douglas (right) was involved in all aspects of life in New Caledonia.

As the new governor of Vancouver Island, James Douglas was worried. American miners were flocking to the island. Not only that, there were several American vessels off the coast of the Queen Charlotte Islands. Worst of all, he'd heard rumours of fighting between the native people and the miners. Law and order must be maintained.

First, he asked Britain to pass a law preventing foreigners from mining the gold in the Queen Charlottes. Britain refused. In 1853, however, Douglas was appointed Lieutenant-Governor of the Queen Charlotte Islands. This meant he could demand that every miner have a license before he searched for gold. It wasn't much, but it would give Douglas more control over what happened in the region.

But Douglas was too late. In a little over two years, the Queen Charlotte gold rush was over. Not one miner applied for a license. Still, the seed had been planted. There was gold in the region called New Caledonia. Lots of it!

Chapter Two

THE WORD GETS OUT

The Native people (seen here near Spence's Bridge) were the first to discover gold.

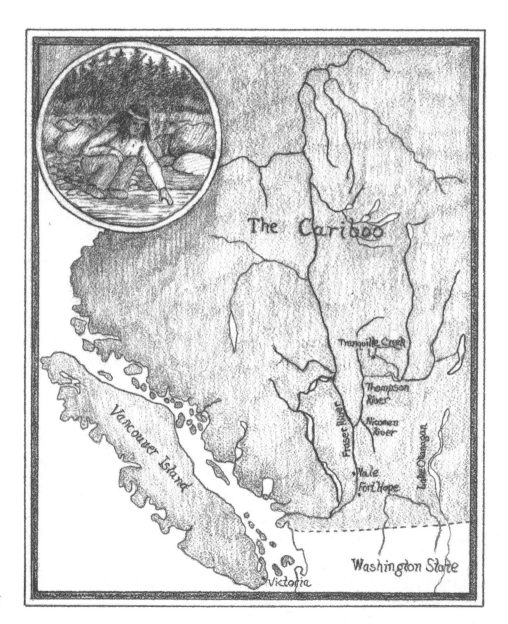

No one knows for sure who found the gold that started the Fraser River gold rush. Some say the Hudson's Bay Company was buying gold from the native people in the Kamloops area as early as 1852. Others maintain that a Scottish sailor first found gold where the Tranquille Creek intersects with the Thompson in 1857. Still another story suggests that a Native person walking on the banks of the Nicomen River stopped for a drink and fished a large gold pebble out of the water.

Whatever story you believe, by 1858 the HBC had acquired 800 ounces of gold. It had acquired it, more than likely, from a variety of sources. And it saw the gold as a new and plentiful resource.

Opportunities

Prospective miners wanting to emigrate from England could find plenty of information in *The Handbook of British Columbia and Emigrant's Guide To The Gold Fields*, published in London. This short reference book told prospective miners all about the new colony and the riches to be found there. It said: "Nowhere is there such a field for adventure and so good an opening for surplus population and struggling enterprise. It is no exaggeration but simple fact that the gold diggings is a lottery in which there are no blanks, and the prizes are indeed splendid. The country is also beautiful, abounding in wood, water and grass. There you can make your own fortune."

If the miner had no luck in the gold fields, the handbook suggested other ways he could make money. He could "cultivate the soil" or he could trade with the miners. "He might find himself happily successful in a beer and spirit store for miners will, in spite of all things, indulge freely in this respect.

"There is a scarcity of unmarried females throughout the colony and no sooner do they arrive than they receive substantial offers of matrimony and future happiness.

"The soil of Vancouver Island is rich and very productive; wheat, potatoes, swedes, turnips, peas, beans, oats and barley thrive remarkably well; and a healthy and nutritious root grows wild in the open prairie, called 'kamass' a favourite food with the natives."

Those who ought to go: capitalists, artisans, mechanics, labourers and able-bodied men of every description. Unmarried females.

Those who ought not to go: persons of a weak constitution, of no particular trade or calling.

If the men had no luck in the gold fields, they could cultivate the productive soil on Vancouver Island.

Packing Up

The list of supplies men should take with them when emigrating to British Columbia:

a strong waterproof coat
two thick blue flannel shirts
a warm pea jacket
waistcoat and trousers to match
a light drill or fustian jacket and trousers
a pilot overcoat
a pair of strong leather braces
three pairs stout worsted stockings or socks
three pairs cotton stockings or socks
six pocket handkerchiefs
one pair boots
one pair highwater boots
six strong loose cotton shirts
one strong felt hat
one light soft hat
three towels
shaving glass, brush and razor
hair brush and comb
two pounds marine soap
one pair blankets
one sheet
a hair bed or mattress and pillow
blacking and brushes
knife and fork
a pint drinking mug
tin bowl and can
one tin plate
tablespoon and teaspoon
a hook pot

Women were advised to take the following:

a thick warm dress
two or three cotton dresses
two or three flannel petticoats
two cotton petticoats
six pocket handkerchiefs
three night caps
six sleeping jackets
one pair stays
six chemises
one light shawl
four caps
two bonnets
a thick warm cloak
three pairs black worsted stockings
six pairs cotton stockings
two pairs boots
six towels

Miners who could afford to buy provisions often shopped in tent stores like this one at Leech River.

Fur returns were falling. The cost of running the company was rising. Gold could bring the company much-needed money. Not only that, it was easy to transport. But first it had to be minted.

James Douglas put the gold on board the *S.S. Otter* and sent the ship to the San Francisco mint. The head of the mint, who was also a member of the volunteer fire department, mentioned the find to a group of his friends. The next big gold rush, he predicted, would be on the banks of the Fraser.

At first, no one paid much attention to this declaration. Only a small group of American prospectors decided to go north and have a look. They left immediately for New Caledonia and arrived on the Fraser in very early spring.

When the miners asked the Hudson's Bay Company for information about the new territory, they didn't learn much. The HBC was tight-lipped: it didn't want newcomers disturbing its fur-trading activity. But a lack of information didn't stop the men from searching for gold.

Disease

Prospectors were advised to "beware of and guard against yellow fever. Sulphate of quinine is a good, and in fact, the best preventative; next to that we would add personal cleanliness, i.e. frequent ablution, and do not be afraid of cold baths if you can get them, for there is no fear of taking cold."

The Motherlode

Many of the miners who began panning between Fort Hope and Fort Yale found soft gold powder that looked like yellow flour when it was crushed. This made them wonder where the motherlode was.

The motherlode is the source of the gold — where the gold comes from. It's usually a vein which contains the gold "in place." Many miners travelling up the Fraser were from California. Their experiences there had taught them that the motherlode was the richest gold source of all. And each of them wanted to be the one to find it.

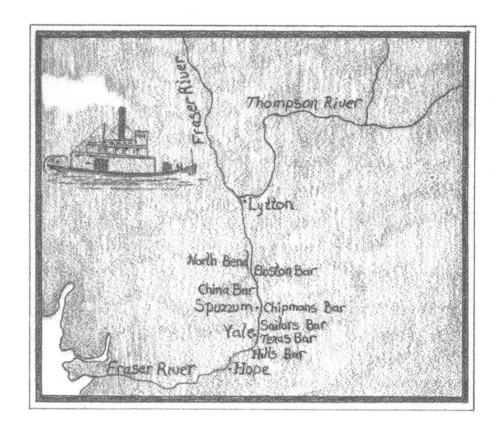

After sending word of their find to San Francisco, the miners continued to dig. On average days they came up with about $50 in gold. On exceptionally good days the take might be closer to $80 or $100. The miners knew they were on to something big — but they had no idea how big it would turn out to be. Eventually, Hill's Bar would yield $2 million in gold.

When the news of Hill's Bar reached San Francisco, the timing couldn't have been better. The California rush was over and the bored miners had nothing better to do than dream of their next big strike. Mills shut down and sailors abandoned their ships. They were off to the Fraser!

A Sleepy Village Transformed

When the gold rush first began, Victoria was little more than a quiet village.

The first book to be published on Vancouver Island was written by Alfred Waddington, a British man who came to the colony to open a grocery store. In his 1858 book *The Fraser Mines Vindicated*, he describes Victoria before the miners arrived:

"On landing we found a quiet village with no bustle, no gamblers, no speculators or interested parties to preach up this or underrate that. There were a few quietly behaved inhabitants, chiefly Scotchmen."

Before too long, however, Waddington would witness this:

"The immigration was so sudden that people had to spend their nights in the streets or bushes, according to their choice, for there were no hotels to receive them. Victoria had at last been discovered and everybody was bound for Victoria.

"Never perhaps was there so large an immigration in so short a space of time into so small a place. Exorbitant prices were asked for goods and the Hudson's Bay store was literally besieged from morning till night. All were in such a hurry that they did not care to wait three or four hours, and sometimes half a day, for his turn to get in.

"Shops, stores and wooden shanties of every description, and in every direction, were now seen going up, and nothing was to be heard but the stroke of the chisel or hammer. In six weeks, 223 buildings, of which nearly 200 were stores, and of these 39 belonging to jobbers or importers, had been added to a village of 800 inhabitants.

"The price of land rose in proportion. Town lots 60 by 120 feet, that had been sold by the Company for fifty and seventy-five dollars, were resold a month afterwards at prices varying from fifteen hundred to three thousand dollars and more. Old town lots, well situated, brought any price and frontages of 20 and 30 feet by 60 deep, rented from 250 to 400 dollars per month."

Those arriving were: "gamblers, swindlers, thieves, drunkards and jail birds let loose by the Governors of California for the benefit of mankind. Mixed up among these, however, was a large body of respectable emigrants; patient, hard-working miners and others; honest men who had come here to live by their industry, hoping to assist their families and better their position."

Men flooded into the British territory. Some decided to travel overland through Oregon and Washington. They arrived in New Caledonia south of Lake Okanagan and travelled up old fur-trading trails to the Thompson River, which they followed to the upper reaches of the Fraser. It was a long, hard journey and it was made even harder because of battles with the native people going on in the area. Instead of going overland, most miners decided to take a ship from San Francisco and enter the new gold colony through Fort Victoria.

A small community of between 300 and 800, Fort Victoria was described by one prospector in 1858 as having "houses that are built of wood and in such a flimsy manner that a hurricane would certainly carry the whole town away."

Ship records from San Francisco show that 455 miners left for Fort Victoria in April, 1,262 in May, 7,149 in June and 6,278 in July. But the records don't tell the real story. There were many more people on board the ships than most people realized. Miners were so anxious to travel that ship owners were taking on as many passengers as they could. One writer estimates that in May, June and July, 23,000 people boarded Victoria-bound boats in San Francisco, while another 8,000 travelled overland.

The rates of passage from San Francisco to Fort Victoria were $65 for first-class steamer, $35 for steerage and $25 to $60 for a large sailboat.

It was near noon on a Sunday in late April when the first group of prospectors disembarked from the ship *Commodore*. Townspeople leaving church stared curiously as the men slowly made their way to shore. They didn't know what to expect. But they were soon to find out. Shiploads of miners began arriving in the small community every day, pitching their tents on the outskirts of the city.

While some men gambled and drank in canvas tents, others spent time in places like the Colonial Hotel before leaving for the gold fields.

Naturalist and veterinarian John Lord was in Victoria at the time. He wrote: "In all directions were canvas tents, from the white strip stretched over a ridge-pole and pegged to the ground (affording just room enough for two to crawl in and sleep), to the great canvas store, a blaze of light, redolent of cigars, smashes, cobblers and cocktails. The rattle of the dice-box, the droning invitation of the keepers of the montetables, the discordant sounds of badly-played instruments, angry words, oaths too terrible to name, roistering songs with noisy refrains, were all signs significant of the gold talisman that met me on every side, as I elbowed my way amidst the unkempt throng, that were waiting for means to take them to the auriferous bars of the far-famed Fraser River."

23

Rough and Ready

Miners carried most of their supplies on their backs.

Rough-looking with their unshaven chins, red flannel shirts and corduroy pants tucked into high boots, the miners were greeted suspiciously when they arrived in Fort Victoria. The packs on their backs were loaded with supplies including blankets, pans, spades and picks. Most of them carried something else: a cartridge belt and a pair of revolvers slung around the waist.

The miners made people nervous. They were thought to be lawless, vicious and irresponsible — a threat to normal, civilized society.

In fact, the miners were glad to be out of lawless California, where violence and thievery ruled. With the exception of the native battles, the new colony was orderly and controlled and that made mining much easier.

By the end of the year, Victoria had grown from a small town of 300 to a thriving city of 3,000. For most men, however, Victoria was simply a stopping-off point—a place to eat, sleep and prepare for the gold fields. Some of those men didn't know they had many more miles to travel before they got to the gold diggings. And before they could even begin the trek up the Fraser, they had to cross the unpredictable waters of the Strait of Georgia.

Still they were determined. Some took canoes, others quickly built simple boats or crude rafts. Personal safety wasn't something they even considered. Getting to the gold was the most important thing of all. But the Strait of Georgia was full of dangerous tides and currents. Many of the men died crossing the water. Others drowned in the river itself.

In May 1858, Governor Douglas wrote: "Boats, canoes and every species of small craft are continually pouring into the Fraser River. Many accidents have happened in the dangerous rapids of the river. A great number of canoes have been dashed to pieces and their cargoes swept away by the impetuous stream, while of the ill-fated adventurers who accompanied them, many have been swept into eternity."

Arriving on the mainland, the men didn't bother with the lowest part of the Fraser. There was little, if any, gold there. But just above Fort Langley, gold began to show up. Most of the men began to pan the fourteen miles between Fort Hope and Fort Yale. Some went a little farther upriver to Boston Bar. They were drawn by names like Texas Bar, China Bar, Murderer's Bar and New York Bar.

After building rough shacks, the miners would use simple equipment like pans and shovels to search for gold. They would examine the sides or banks closest to the river. After that, they'd branch out and look at the gravel banks further away. The miners referred to the workings on the rivers and their banks as "bars."

A few of the more daring prospectors headed even further up the Fraser towards Lytton. But the dangers weren't over yet. They had to be on the continual lookout for native warriors, who were scattered in pockets along the way, waiting to attack. Along with that, food and supplies were hard to get, and those that the men could find were ridiculously expensive.

One Miner's Story

Edward (Ned) Stout continued mining into his late '80s.

Ned Stout was one of a group of Californians who made it to the Fraser in May of 1858. Stout arrived just in time to fight a running battle with the native people.

The native people had owned the land long before the Europeans came, and they weren't pleased to see the miners digging in their rivers and building lean-tos along their banks. For one thing, they believed the miners' presence would drive the salmon away. For another, they were used to being paid for their furs. Now they wanted to be paid for their gold. They decided to fight back and reclaim their land.

As Stout and twenty-five of his friends struggled through the thick forest along the Fraser, they befriended a young native girl. One night she appeared by the fire and warned them to leave.

"Before sunup you white men go. Go back in the stick, far, far back to the water. Indian kill all white men in canyon, by-by he come kill you all. Tomorrow he come. Go now. Go quick."

Taking her advice, Stout and his friends immediately packed up their things and, using the moon to light their way, began to travel quickly back down the Fraser. But they were not fast enough for the native people.

Using arrows poisoned with rattlesnake venom, the native warriors attacked. Even a nick from a poisoned arrow would cause convulsions and eventually turn a body black. As Stout recalled many years later, they lost a man nearly every day.

By the time Stout was hit, the native warriors were out of venom. His seven arrow wounds, though dangerous, would eventually heal. Of the twenty-six men who had left California together, only four survived the native attacks.

Eventually the miners decided to take action against the native people. They held a meeting at Fort Yale and formed a volunteer police force. A large group of them, armed with rifles, made their way back up the canyon where the native people were waiting. The show of force impressed the native warriors, and in August of 1858 peace treaties were signed with all the tribes between Yale and Lytton.

Not all prospectors found gold. One man who became discouraged and returned home was Robert Frost of Oregon. He describes conditions in a letter to a friend:

"Provisions began to run short and then it took all we could make to live. We had to pay $1.00 per pound for everything, flour, bacon and beans, all alike. There was none to be bought at any price so one evening a half a dozen of us took an inventory of what we had, and it looked so scaly that we packed up next morning, left our tools, got into my canoe and started down the river. My stock in trade, outside of the canoe, consisted of my blankets, about four pounds of salt pork, and $12.00 in gold dust. We made Boston Bar that afternoon, beached the canoe as we could not take it through the canyon, we started up the mountain; night overtook us and we had to sleep in the snow. About nine o'clock next morning we made Lake House on the trail, a mere shack, where the proprietor got us up a breakfast at $1.00 each. It consisted of hard tack, bacon and beans with a raw onion. I thought at that time it was the best breakfast I had ever eaten."

Yale

Traces of the gold boom still remain in Yale, now a small village with just a few businesses and houses. At one time, Yale was the destination point for sternwheelers, mules and freight wagons. They would drop supplies for the thousands of men who were either mining between Yale and Hope or heading up country to the Cariboo gold fields. Millions of dollars in gold poured through the town, which in the early days was little more than a village with two streets, a handful of cottages, two churches and about twenty saloons and stores.

Twice the town was almost totally destroyed by fire, once in July 1880 and again in August 1881. Both times, Yale was rebuilt. By the summer of 1882, it was the meeting place for almost ten thousand men hired to build the Canadian Pacific Railway.

Today, foundations of a few old buildings can still be seen along the former waterfront, while Hill's Bar, downstream from Yale on the east bank of the Fraser, is visible when the water is low.

One of the wealthiest men living in Yale was a rough but honest Yankee collier known as "Old York." He had left the American coal mines to prospect for gold in British Columbia. When he arrived in Yale he realized the community was in an ideal location. Instead of spending his time searching for gold, he opened a store and bought as much of the surrounding land as he could afford. Even though he became a very rich man, he was a colourful character who continued to dress as a poor collier in an open-necked buttonless blue shirt, thick boots and tight moleskin pants that reached far short of the ankles.

Miners lining up for licenses in the late 1890s. This building still stands in Victoria today.

As the men hurried to the gold fields, Governor Douglas was busy trying to retain order. The possibility of war between the native people and the prospectors was growing. Not only that, while many of the men were law abiding and orderly, some were not. When he learned that speculators were taking possession of land, staking out lots for sale, and travelling in unlicensed canoes, Douglas stepped in. Though he had legal jurisdiction over Vancouver Island only, someone had to take control of the mainland territory. Douglas decided to do it. He moved quickly to establish mining regulations and made each prospector pay five dollars a year for a mining license.

That first rush up the Fraser was short-lived. It lasted just a few months and peaked in June of 1858. Most of the men who had initially rushed to the Fraser called it a "great humbug." Disgruntled with the native people, the costs and the transportation problems, they went home.

About 3,000 men stayed behind. But even they stopped panning for gold. They had to. Like it did every year in late spring, the Fraser River flooded. The gold banks were covered with water. The men who stayed behind were the determined ones, however. They weren't about to give up that easily. They returned to Fort Victoria and waited for the water to recede. They wanted another crack at the lucky Fraser!

Chapter Three

GETTING TO THE GOLD

It was late summer, 1858. The water on the Fraser was beginning to fall. The gold bars were becoming accessible again. While many disgruntled miners had returned home, others were determined to strike it rich. Hill's Bar was still being worked and so were dozens of others. Conditions, however, were appalling, particularly the "big canyon" stretch north of Yale to Lytton.

James Douglas was worried. He knew all about the terrible travelling conditions the men had to endure to reach their destinations. Miners described trails littered with dead horses and thick with inches of mud. In some spots there was barely a trail at all; men were forced to move forward by clinging to the sides of mountains.

Gearing Up

An English writer, Kinahan Cornwallis, described a typical miner:

"He was a gaunt, stringy, dried up looking Kentuckian, with a gutta-percha coloured face, sunk into which, on either side of his nose, twinkled two all alive and piercing eyes. His hair was long and light, and crisped up with the dry heat of the weather, so much so that it gave me the idea of extreme fragility and brittleness. He carried a couple of revolvers and a bowie knife, with the point of which he took the opportunity of picking his teeth immediately after supper."

Many publications of the day suggested what miners should take to the gold fields. Each list differed slightly, but the basics included:

* miner's license
* gold pan
* good-quality axe
* miner's pick (In East Kootenay country, on Wild Horse and Perry creeks, the miners used a pick that was sharpened on one end and had a hammer head on the other. In most other areas, miners preferred a "two-pound" pick head with a protective steel shank)
* a round-nosed shovel
* tall, sturdy rubber boots
* packboard or packsack to carry supplies
* small bottle for storing gold
* matches, compass and a strong waterproof container for them
* area map and notebook
* curved tweezers (optional) for taking gold from the pan or cracks in bedrock
* stiff whisk (optional) for brushing bedrock dirt into a pan
* a small magnet
* a good sleeping bag or a pair of double blankets
* a tent or 7 x 9 canvas sheet
* aluminum or tin cooking pots and an enamel cup
* soap, bandages, iodine and a few "simple" medicines

Rough-looking with unshaven chins and gaunt faces, the miners endured tough conditions to get to the gold fields.

Alfred Waddington had a friend who went to the gold fields beyond Yale, along the upper Fraser. "He has since related to me the fatigues and miseries he had to endure, when creeping through underwood and thickets for miles, sometimes on his hands and knees, with a bag of flour on his back, under fallen trees or over them, scrambling up precipices, then sliding down again over sharp stony ground, or through bogs and swamps. As the adventurers trod their weary way onward every day more exhausted and way worn, each little caravan became smaller and smaller, according as one or the other lagged behind to rest, or turned back in despair. Tired and almost ready to drop, they would come to a likely piece of property to prospect, but nobody had the inclination to do it."

Panning

William Hind's painting, "Victoria," 1862, depicts the artists' admiration for the way of life of the Cariboo gold miners.

The first thing a miner did when he reached his site was prospect. Unstrapping his gold pan from his back, he filled it with a shovelful of sand and gravel and then carefully dipped it into the river or stream. It was important that he filled it with slow-moving or still water. If the water moved too fast, it carried away the earth and the miner would have to start over. Once he had enough water, he'd lift the pan out, turn it in a circle and stir the contents with his hand until everything was good and wet.

Gently working his fingers through the gravel, the miner broke up bits of clay and threw away any large pebbles or stones. His stirring also had another purpose.

It allowed the gold, which is six times heavier than regular rock, to sink to the bottom of the pan.

Working very carefully, the miner tilted the gold pan away from his body so that the water carried the lighter material over the lip and onto the ground. Again he filled the pan with water, again he swished it and gently poured off the lighter sand or earth. He did this over and over again until the gravel was almost all gone. But he had to be careful because, in the process, he could pour away a gold nugget or bits of fine gold. Finally, all that remained in the pan was a few spoonfuls of black or metallic sand and — if he was lucky — gold!

Equipment

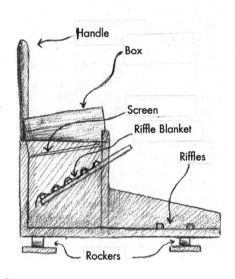

Handle

Box

Screen

Riffle Blanket

Riffles

Rockers

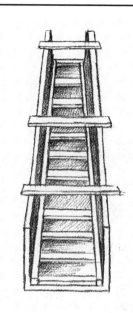

A typical **gold pan** was about eighteen inches wide, three or four inches deep and had broad, sloping sides. Some people think the first gold pan was used by miners in Transylvania as far back as the fifteenth century – and possibly even earlier.

Some miners used a **rocker** instead of a gold pan. The rocker box was sometimes called a "cradle" or "dolly." It allowed the men to wash large amounts of sand and gravel all at once. Rockers were wooden boxes with screens on top. Gravel was placed on the top screen and water was poured onto the gravel. Men usually worked rockers in pairs: as one poured water onto the gravel, another would rock the box from side to side. This would send the fine sand to the lower part of the box, while the gold would be caught on a series of riffles or aprons in the very bottom of the box.

The **sluice box** was like the rocker, only longer and much heavier. Sluices couldn't be moved easily, so they were usually built once prospectors found gold and decided an area was worth mining. The sluice box worked much like the rocker. The miners would set it up near a "gold creek." Once water was running through the sluice, they would start shovelling gravel into the box. Again, the fine sand was washed away while the gold was caught in the riffles.

By 1858, more than five hundred men were located within eight miles of Fort Hope.

In spite of tough travelling conditions, men were still finding the time and the energy to pan. Over 500 men were located within eight miles of Fort Hope. At this point, most of the prospectors were working the bars and doing "surface" digging. They were only going down about fifteen inches. Just about all of them were finding between an ounce and a half and six and a half ounces of gold every day. Some used gold pans. Others used small rockers. A few set up bigger sluices.

Even though he wasn't legally allowed to do it, Douglas decided to offer a deal to the miners. He told them his government was prepared to give them transportation, food and equipment in exchange for the labour needed to build a proper mule trail through the mountains to Lillooet. The route would by-pass the rough terrain of the Fraser Canyon by going up Harrison River and Harrison Lake, rejoining the Fraser at Lillooet.

To encourage the miners to stick with the job, he demanded a twenty-five dollar deposit from each of them, to be reimbursed in goods when they reached Lillooet. The miners thought it was a great deal. Sure they had to work, but in the process they could get to the mines for nothing and be fed along the way.

Five hundred men were taken to the head of Harrison Lake in two groups. Digging started, but the work went slowly. There weren't enough

Harrison-Lillooet Trail

By the time the Harrison-Lillooet Trail was finished, goods were transported from Port Douglas.

When the Harrison-Lillooet Trail was finished, *The Victoria Gazette* praised the new route and said that goods could be transported from Port Douglas at the head of Harrison Lake to Lillooet at just eighteen cents a pound, compared to over forty-six cents a pound on the Fraser Canyon trails. Unfortunately, the Harrison-Lillooet Trail builders didn't do as good a job as people initially thought. The men had built the trails along dry creek beds, which became impassable when the spring floods came. They even built the bridges too low and an officer of the Hudson's Bay Company predicted that "most of them will be swept away during the next freshets."

mules to help, and as the trail got tougher, half the men had to carry provisions for the other half. Some men became discouraged, sold their tickets and left. Others, getting their fill of pork and beans, stayed on. The Harrison Trail, which was four feet wide, was finished in five months and was one of the first roads into the B.C. interior.

As the men completed their contract, they wanted their provisions delivered — preferably at the upper end of the trail. It wasn't to be. As a compromise, they had to walk halfway back down the trail — seventy miles — to get what was owed to them. In spite of the disgruntled miners, the trail was opened. It would remain open all winter, which meant miners could stay on the upper Fraser year-round if they wanted to.

Officials in Britain praised Douglas for taking the initiative—first for issuing licenses for the miners and now for organizing a trail. They listened carefully when he spoke of his concerns about organizing the mainland territory. Finally, they offered him the governorship of the mainland as well, and in November of 1858, the province of British Columbia was formed. One of Douglas's first steps after being sworn in was to appoint Matthew Baillie Begbie judge of the new territory.

Begbie, who became known as the hanging judge, was a particularly colourful character. Roaming the country with a string of twelve horses (he called it "going on circuit"), Begbie always managed to appear at the first sign of trouble, don his robes and hold court on the spot—in cabins, barns, tents, saloons, even in his saddle.

The Hanging Judge

Sir Matthew Baillie Begbie

Sir Matthew Baillie Begbie wasn't called the hanging judge for nothing. He was given the nickname because so many men were hanged after being convicted in his court. Even so, he was fair. He never hanged a man the jury did not convict (back then, hanging was the only penalty for murder).

He was a no-nonsense man and just about everyone was scared of him—criminals and honest citizens alike. For one thing, he was big. He was six feet, five inches tall. For another, he was dramatic-looking, with a sharp, pointed moustache and a Van Dyke beard. But it was his stern, no-nonsense manner and the blunt way he spoke that scared people most of all. In sentencing a man to eighteen months for robbing a church poor-box, he yelled:

"When you come out, never shake an honest man by the hand—never look an honest man in the face! Go to the other side of the world where you are not known. Should you be so unwise as to stay in this country and should your form again throw its shadow in the courthouse charged with crime, and you are found guilty, and I am sitting on this bench, I will send you to a place where you will speak to your fellow man no more!"

And Begbie wasn't above threatening a group of men at Wild Horse Creek who *hadn't* broken the law.

In spite of being called the hanging judge, Begbie (seated at left) was considered fair by just about everyone who knew him.

"Boys, I am here to keep order and to administer the law. Those who don't want law and order can git, but those who stay within the camp remember on which side of the line the camp is. For boys, if there is shooting in Kootenay, there will be hanging in Kootenay."

As well as writing about his court activities, Begbie also found the time to make notes about the land, the living conditions and the men he encountered. He also wrote about money that could be made in each area and likely routes for new roads. Almost all of this information was passed on to Governor Douglas.

Though Begbie worked hard, had high standards and stuck to the rules, he wasn't afraid to take the law into his own hands from time to time. In a hotel room in Clinton, for example, he once heard friends of a man he had just sentenced plotting to kill him. The judge listened for a while and then, with absolute disgust, emptied his chamberpot over them.

Begbie was made Chief Justice of British Columbia in 1870 and was knighted in 1875. He was one of the few men to stand up for the Chinese against the oppressive policies of the British Columbia government.

This unidentified sternwheeler was one of many that travelled the waters near Hope during gold rush times.

By the time Begbie was enforcing the law, prospectors arriving in Fort Victoria didn't have to borrow canoes or build boats to get up the Fraser. Quick-thinking American skippers had brought their paddle-wheelers north and, for about twenty dollars, were offering people regular trips to Fort Hope. One of the first ships to make the trip was the sidewheeler *Surprise*. A reporter with *The San Francisco Bulletin* witnessed the arrival of that first trip:

"After supper and a smoke, watches being settled (against Indian attack) we got under the blankets and were talking, when one of the party exclaimed that he heard the sound of paddlewheels. In an instant we were on our feet and listening. There was no doubting it. As the steamer neared us with her lights shining out in the darkness, our camp was in about as excited a state as could be imagined. Along she came until abreast our fire, when the anchor dropped and in two minutes I was aboard the *Surprise* whilst the party ashore were saluting her with guns and revolvers. She had left Fort Langley at 7½ PM and had made twenty miles in two hours, the current running about six knots against her. The next morning, the 6th, at 3½ AM, she went ahead, and at 2 PM arrived at Fort Hope."

It took the *Surprise* twenty-four hours to make the trip from Victoria to Fort Hope. Going back was faster—it took only fifteen and a half hours. But being a sidewheeler, the *Surprise* didn't have the power needed to handle the currents on the Fraser well enough to make it all the way to Yale. A sternwheeler by the name of *Umatilla* did, and a few months after the *Surprise* made her first trip, the *Umatilla* was the first steamboat to make a rough and rocky trip from Fort Langley all the way to the mouth of the Fraser Canyon. The trip was too dangerous to repeat and it would be a little while longer before Yale would become a regular destination point for more powerful sternwheelers.

Steamboats were getting through, and now that the Harrison-Lillooet Trail was open, packers were beginning to operate as well. These men would load up their mule trains with supplies and, braving bad weather and poor travelling conditions, make it through the wilderness to bring food and equipment to the miners.

Paying Up!

The cost of getting provisions to the gold camps was ridiculously high. For instance, a barrel of flour that sold for $16 at Bellingham Bay cost $25 at Fort Langley, $36 at Hope and $100 at Sailor's Bar. One miner said, "At Fort Hope there was nothing to be had but dried salmon. At Fort Langley plenty of black flour at 9 dollars a hundred and salt salmon, four for 1 dollar. What lively visions of scurvy these provisions conjure up!"

A reporter for *The New York Times* said, "Canoes are very scarce; the price has risen from 50 dollars and 80 dollars to 100 dollars each."

The prospectors appreciated the changes that time was bringing, but they were still intent on one thing: finding gold. Unfortunately, winter had arrived, bringing with it colder weather. One miner, writing to his sister in California, said, "I was all alone in a cotton tent for two months. I worked hard—would not speak to one for perhaps ten days together. Have even slept out many nights under a tree with nothing but a blanket over me. We suffered considerably."

With the low water in the spring of 1859, the miners began to push northward. The rush that had started on the lower Fraser had taken men to the Thompson and Similkameen rivers and to countless streams beyond. Men were making as much as twenty, thirty, even forty dollars a day and the gold was getting coarser.

Certain they were getting closer to the motherlode—and a major gold find—men were also looking up from the gravel and powder found along the riverbeds to the looming hills above the Fraser. It was here, as one writer put it, that "layers of gold-bearing rocks were spread like secret jam."

This was the gold Ned Stout and many others were looking for. About the same time Stout headed north, a group of Americans led by Peter Dunlevy followed him. Dunlevy was accompanied by four companions, who made it as far as the mouth of the Chilcotin River. There, they met a native individual who promised to take them to a river where "gold lay like beans in a pan."

A few days later the men were led through the wilderness to the Horsefly River—and their gold nuggets. Other miners paid little attention to the find. But the excited men didn't care. There was enough gold to keep them busy for quite a while. What Dunlevy and his friends didn't realize was that they were the first men to find gold in what would become the richest gold region in British Columbia—the Cariboo!

Amateurs and Experts

According to one witness, "an amateur could discover gold on the Fraser, whereas it required experience and skill to prospect for gold in the mountains." Much of the gold in the Cariboo was below ground and required heavy digging, while the gold on the Fraser was often in the beds or along riverbanks and much easier for gold panners to get at.

The type of gold also varied from area to area. Sometimes it was round and jagged, other times it was smooth and oblong like seeds. Occasionally it appeared as coarse, rough lumps. Its colour varied, too—some gold was an iron-rust colour, some was pale silvery, some bronze-yellow and some the glittering yellow that you'd expect.

Chapter Four

TO THE CARIBOO!

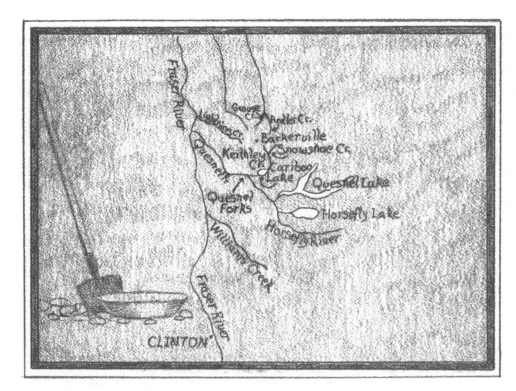

This miner's cabin in the Cariboo is more sophisticated than most. Many were nothing more than lean-to shacks.

Northward, northward! By 1860, word had filtered south that gold was being discovered around Cariboo Lake and Horsefly River. The strikes were rich. Rumour had it that some men were making over $100 a day! That was all the motivation the miners needed. They believed the further into the interior they pushed, the heavier and larger the gold would be. And the more money they would make.

As soon as the weather broke in the spring of 1860, the miners began to explore the creeks and streams feeding the lakes. George Weaver and W.R. (Doc) Keithley came across a creek that flowed into Cariboo Lake from the north. Quickly christening the stream "Keithley" after Doc Keithley, they began to test the gravel. They struck gold!

As the *British Colonist* of Victoria reported shortly afterwards, seventy buckets of "dirt" yielded $140, an excellent return. Soon gold was discovered in several other nearby creeks. Excitement began to build. The community of Keithley sprang up almost overnight.

Filling Up

Hunger was a very real problem for miners in the Cariboo. Some men weren't making enough money to buy supplies, which were terribly overpriced. Flour, bacon, beans and salt were $1.50 a pound, while dried apples were $2.50 a pound. In many cases when the miners did have money, there were no supplies to be bought because there weren't enough mules bringing in provisions. Nevertheless, men continued to order food and many of them based their orders on the guidelines listed in the publication *Prospecting in Canada*. The basics were:

flour or hardtack	sugar
baking powder	tea
oatmeal	coffee
beans	chocolate
rice	onions, dried
evaporated potatoes	barley
split peas	powdered milk
dried soup vegetables	salt
bacon and ham	dried fruit
lard	pepper
cheese	spices
crystallized eggs	butter
beef tea capsules	

The publication also said that mustard, jam, yeast-cakes, spices, syrup, macaroni, cornmeal, pickles, molasses, corned beef and ketchup could be added according to taste.

Many men could only dream of food. Some carried rifles and tried to shoot wild game. Others were prepared to work for food instead of money. And some became more preoccupied with finding food than finding gold.

"It is a fact that we saw a crowd of men standing around a butcher's slaughter-house waiting for the offal of a bullock to be thrown amongst them. This they seized like a pack of hounds." W. Champness

This store is well stocked, but many communities offered little more than dried salmon or black flour.

"Keithley," one weary miner recalled some time after he arrived, "is one of the most dull and gloomy places on the route, consisting of rude log-shanties of the roughest description. The little stock of provisions we had brought with us (of beans, bacon and flour) was eagerly bid for by the store-keepers. Not one pound of flour was now obtainable at Keithley, except that which we had brought. Beans and bacon were here 'the staff of life.'"

Weaver and Keithley worked hard opening up the creek, hoping it might lead to great riches. They had some success, but in the fall of 1860 they decided to explore further. The weather had already turned cold; travelling conditions were difficult. Nevertheless, Weaver, Keithley and two companions worked their way northwest along Keithley Creek and up Snowshoe Creek to its source. Carefully they made their way over the mountains to untouched valleys. Finally, they reached a creek that flowed through a narrow, rock canyon. It was Antler Creek. And it would soon be famous.

Without even digging, one man bent down and took out a pan of gold worth $75. Just as easily, another man removed $100 worth of gold. The men were ecstatic. They had stumbled onto an "eldorado" creek and they were the only ones who knew about it!

Bedding down for the night, the men discussed what they had to do over the next days and weeks. As well as retrieving the gold and building a cabin, they had to bring in supplies to get them through what was probably going to be a very cold winter. When they woke the next morning there was fresh snow on the ground and plenty of work to do.

Two men decided to stay behind and start on the cabin while two others headed back to Keithley for provisions.

Pay Dirt!

"The accounts of gold discoveries at Cariboo are perfectly fabulous and, at the same time, quite true. Large fortunes have been made in a few weeks, from £6,000 to £10,000 earned in a month or six weeks; many instances have occurred of £90 of gold being washed out of a tin pan full of earth. Old miners say they never saw anything like it in the best days of California in '49 and '50. Cariboo is a dreadful place to get at, however, right up in the mountains ...and inaccessible for 7 or 8 months out of the year from snow."

Diary entry by Lieut. Wilson, secretary of the British Boundary Commission

More than anything else, they were determined to keep their find a secret! But while casually ordering their supplies at "Red-headed" Davis's store, somehow their secret leaked out. No one is sure how it happened. Some say it was a single word casually dropped that acted as a clue. Others say it was the way the men acted that tipped the others off.

Whatever it was, as they left the store dozens of other miners on snowshoes stampeded back through the freshly fallen snow to Antler Creek with them. Within days, the entire creek was heavily staked. So much excitement was stirred up that claims were staked over claims and disputes broke out. Many of the men held their ground by living in huts or holes in the snow right on their claims.

Little Irritants

They weren't as dangerous as the bears the men had to watch out for, but they were far more irritating. They were mosquitoes, and much to the miners' dismay, they flourished in the Cariboo. "On the fourth night we had consumed all our stock of provisions except tea, of which we had brought a good supply. We were now weary, anxious, hungry, without food and irritated to desperation by the mosquitoes. After making tea, which was some refreshment, we tried to sleep, but could not, in consequence of our blood-sucking tormentors. Long before morning we arose, lighted fires around ourselves in all directions, lay down again, and, covering heads and faces with our blankets, obtained some measure of repose." W. Champness

Miners were encouraged to travel with "fly oil." Though they could try simple oil of pine needles to keep the bugs away, this mixture was supposed to be far better:

1 pint pine tar
1½ pints olive or sweet oil
1 ounce citronella
½ ounce carbolic acid

Meanwhile, miners just a day or two behind the first rush found much of the rich ground already taken. They were forced to go on further or take on new streams to try to find gold. A group of men, William Dietz, Michael Burns and Vital La Force, pushed up the creek and prospected through seven and eight feet of snow. Dietz tried panning. At first he found nothing. But, after discovering a bare bedrock outcropping, he came up with gold at a dollar to the pan. His companions weren't terribly impressed, but Dietz thought he was on to something. The creek, which would eventually become the most famous in the Cariboo, was named Williams Creek after Dietz.

Dietz and his companions, including Ned Stout, worked hard over the next few months clearing the land and, as the snow melted, dealing with the rising water in the creek. But most people weren't impressed with Williams Creek. Other creeks in the area—Lightning, Lowhee and Grouse—seemed more promising. And over the next few years those three creeks *would* yield a tremendous amount of gold. But Dietz, Stout and the others weren't about to give up their Williams claims.

In his memoirs, Ned Stout remembered finding gold on Williams Creek:

"Our discovery claim was in the canyon, and was called Stout's Gulch. At the depth of a few feet the gold had a totally different colour to what it had at greater depth. The shallower gold

Stout's Gulch, which was named for Ned Stout, who staked the first claim in the area.

was dark, while the deep gold was bright, jagged and more valuable."

Even though most people were calling Williams the "humbug creek," Stout's find drew attention. That attention would grow stronger with a discovery made by William Jordan. One morning, while partners John Dawson and Joel Abbott were off getting supplies, Jordan dug down and found unbelievably large, smooth nuggets of gold. He had struck pay dirt! When his partners returned, he showed them the find: almost fifty ounces of gold worth close to $3,000.

47

Transporting Gold

Finding gold was tough enough, but it was even tougher for the men to get their gold safely out of the mining camps and not have it stolen en route. Many men were robbed of their precious gold dust and nuggets while travelling from the camps to Victoria.

Governor Douglas decided to bring in gold escorts. These people travelled with the gold to keep it safe. On horseback and with guns for protection, the dozen men looked important. But most of the miners didn't care about appearances. They wanted nothing to do with the escorts. The reason: gold could be lost or stolen just as

easily with the escorts as it could be without them. And if the gold was lost, the government would not replace it.

After three trips from the Cariboo to the Fraser, the gold escort was finished. The men weren't about to take any chances with their hard-won treasure. Instead they found all sorts of places to hide their gold. They stashed it under the floor of their cabins or beneath trees in the forest. Some men refused to part with it and constantly carried it with them until they had a chance to make the risky trip to Victoria themselves.

The Chinese Influence

The gold rush attracted men from all over the world—including men from China. And although they would be greeted with great hostility, the Chinese miners would play a major role in opening British Columbia to the rest of Canada.

They began to arrive when word of the Fraser gold finds leaked out. They were still coming when the Cariboo rush began. The New Westminster reverend Edward White commented on this in July 1860:

"The Chinese are still coming into the Colony in great numbers. Within the last two weeks over 700 have arrived, and others are on the way. Some come from California, but the greater portion come direct from China...Leading Chinese merchants say that we shall have 50,000 from their country in British Columbia before two years are passed."

Unfortunately, the Chinese — or "Celestials" as they were called — were treated poorly. They were yelled at and sometimes even physically attacked. When it came to gold panning, they were forced to work areas that were already abandoned or areas that were less profitable. When the larger mining companies took over, the Celestials

Chinese miners were willing to work for less money than European miners.

were willing to work for less money than the European miners. This resulted in more bad feelings between the two groups. Because of the poor treatment they received, the Celestials stayed together as a group, didn't mix much with the other miners and were very quiet about what they were doing. But, in spite of the abuse, they stayed in the region.

A small Chinatown sprouted in Victoria—the first in Canada. Another community developed in Quesnel. Here and in places like Barkerville, Chinese men opened businesses like laundries and restaurants. Their services were used, but people still treated them poorly.

As the gold rush waned, the economy suffered and jobs became tougher to find. People began to complain more and more about the influx of Chinese. There were several calls to stop their immigration. But then work began on the Canadian Pacific railroad. Knowing how hard the Chinese miners had worked, officials decided to take advantage of the men to build the railroad. Chinese labourers were imported and they *did* work long and hard—for very little money. Many of them didn't survive. To this day, no one knows for sure how many Chinese men died building the railroad.

The richness of the Jordan strike spread like a fairy tale. Williams Creek was flooded with men hoping for similar luck. And in many, many cases, the miners *were* lucky. They began to count their gold in pounds rather than ounces. For a while, Williams Creek yielded $10,000 a day. The Jordan strike returned almost $250,000 in gold. Official records of the time suggest $2.5 million worth of gold was found in the area in 1861 alone. Since many men didn't claim their finds, the actual take could have been closer to $5 million.

The Cariboo was big news all over British Columbia and beyond. Men were leaving their diggings on the Fraser, diggings that were producing some gold, to go to the Cariboo to strike it rich. And they weren't alone. A gold rush to rival the Fraser brought men from all over the world. Overlanders came from Eastern Canada. More men arrived from the United States. Many more came from Britain and Europe.

The biggest finds of all, however, were still almost a year away. They would be discovered by a sailor named Billy Barker and a man from Ontario named John Cameron. And almost overnight, towns would be established in their names: Camerontown and Barkerville.

The wash-up for one day alone on the Aurora claim — just downstream from Barkerville — was 485 ounces of gold.

Digging Deep

By the time the miners reached the Cariboo, gold mining had changed significantly from those early days on the Fraser. There was more to it than gold pans and small rockers. In fact, James Douglas had noticed the change a year earlier on a visit to Fort Yale. Even then, sluices were more common than rockers, and flumes and ditches were getting longer. In some spots the ditches went on for more than two miles.

The rugged Cariboo would make the change complete. In that area, simple creek panning or surface digging wouldn't turn up much gold. To get at pay dirt, miners had to go fifty or even sixty feet below ground. This was called sinking a shaft. It was expensive work and in many cases miners joined together, pooling their money and their labour to reach their gold mine. Once the shaft was sunk, waterwheels were used to pump water out of the ground. Sometimes as much as twenty million gallons a day of water was removed. But, as one miner remembered, even with all the labour and expense, gold wasn't always discovered.

"The mine proprietors have necessarily to incur excessive expense in the erection of flumes, the carrying out of sluice-boxes, and the sinking of shafts; and many have made this outlay in vain, not succeeding in striking on the right place for the precious deposit. Hundreds have sunk their 'bottom dollar' before reaching the golden ore."

The Cornish Hydra claim on Williams Creek.

51

Chapter Five

CARIBOO BONANZA

Billy Barker

He was a stubborn little English sailor who loved adventure. Lured by tales of the Cariboo, Billy Barker deserted his British ship and arrived on Williams Creek in August 1862. With his bushy salt-and-pepper beard, his love of wine, women and song and his slightly bow-legged walk, he stood out from the other miners immediately.

Except for a few friends, all the men thought he was crazy, especially when he picked out a spot below the canyon on Williams Creek. The area above the canyon was fully staked and producing hundreds of pounds of gold. But nobody had bothered to go down below. Everybody knew there was no gold there.

Billy Barker wasn't so sure. He decided to look for himself.

Finding an old outcropping of rock, Barker believed the creek had run through the area at one time and had probably left gold. Ignoring the taunts and laughter of the other miners, Barker and a few others went to work. They constructed a shafthouse and started digging. They went ten feet. No gold. Twenty feet. Nothing. Thirty feet, then forty. Still no gold. Fifty feet. No gold.

The others were getting discouraged. But not Barker. Apparently he'd had a dream, the same dream over and over again. The dream kept telling him "pay at fifty-two." He urged his friends to keep digging. His instincts, and his dream, were right on. The pay-off came at fifty-two feet. With the turn of a shovel, a square foot of gravel turned up an amount of gold worth $1,000. It made Billy Barker a rich, rich man. Eventually his claim would be worth more than $600,000. It was an unbelievable amount in those days, and it would go down as the biggest bonanza of the Cariboo gold rush.

Squandered Riches

Originally an English potter, Billy Barker abandoned his trade for a love of the sea. Travelling from England, he heard all about the riches to be discovered in a new land called the Cariboo. That, coupled with his strange dream of striking it rich, encouraged him to head for the gold fields. The rest, as they say, is history. But whatever happened to the man who had a town named after him? Unfortunately, he was destined to lose his fortune and die in poverty.

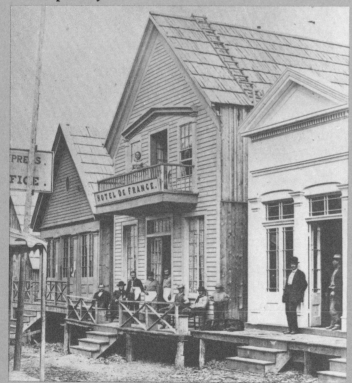

Many miners squandered their riches in places like the Hotel de France.

The winter after Billy Barker struck gold, he decided to follow the lead of some of the other miners and head to Victoria for Christmas. It was a trip that would change his life. There he met and married Elizabeth Collyer. Not too much is known about Mrs. Barker — except for one thing. She loved to have a good time, especially in the gold camps where men outnumbered women 250 to one. And with so many other men paying attention to his new wife, Barker found it difficult to keep up. He began to spend. And spend. And spend some more. Thousands of dollars went to friends and down-and-out miners, much was spent in saloons, but most of the money went to his new wife.

It didn't last. Eventually, Barker's money ran out. And, as soon as it disappeared, his wife disappeared too. By 1866, Billy Barker was ready to leave Barkerville. His friends joined together and paid his stage fare out of town. For close to thirty years, little was heard about the stubborn Englishman. Apparently he cooked in a few mining camps, did whatever odd jobs he could find to survive and continued to do some gold prospecting.

By the spring of 1894, however, Barker was in the news again. This time, the *Victoria Colonist* reported, "William Barker, the old Cariboo miner for whom Barkerville was named, is seriously ill at the old men's home of a cancer which infilters his left jaw, the left side of his neck and his left shoulder."

That summer, at the age of 75, Billy Barker died. He was buried in a pauper's unmarked grave in Victoria's Ross Bay Cemetery. Almost seventy years later, in July 1962, a group of old-time miners and dignitaries unveiled a headstone for Billy Barker's grave.

Miners working the Barker claim. Billy Barker is thought to be the man on the extreme right.

Celebrations began almost instantly. All the miners who had laughed at Billy Barker earlier weren't laughing anymore. They rushed to stake the land next to the Barker claim. Fights broke out as men scrambled to pull up existing stakes and drive their own into the ground. Holes and tunnels were dug; waterwheels were put up. Shanties or shacks were quickly built down either side of a narrow eighteen-foot-wide street. Those shanties had to be built at least two feet above the ground, since water from the creek often flooded the area as the miners worked. Billy Barker's mine produced almost $600,000 in its first year. In honour of the stubborn little Englishman, the miners called the community "Barkerville."

Not long after Barker's claim began to pay off, a clerk from Ontario arrived on Williams Creek. John (Cariboo) Cameron was as different from Billy Barker as black is from white.

Cameron was quieter, happily married, stable. But, wanting to give his wife and infant daughter more than he could afford on his clerk's salary, he decided to try his luck in the gold fields. Cameron's wife, Sophia, wouldn't let her husband travel from Ontario to British Columbia alone. She insisted on travelling the entire 12,000 miles with Cameron. From the east coast they travelled by boat to Panama, up to San Francisco, through to Victoria and, finally, to the Cariboo. Unfortunately, just after arriving in Victoria, their fourteen-month-old daughter became sick and died.

Grimly determined, John and Sophia carried on and arrived at Williams Creek in late August, just a little while after the Barker claim had been discovered. Believing they could have just as much luck as Barker, Cameron and a group of friends staked ground downstream from the Barker claim.

They worked long and hard through the fall, but unfortunately they turned up no gold. Twenty-eight-year-old Sophia Cameron, meanwhile, contracted typhoid fever. Despite help from a local doctor, she died in October. Ultimately, she would be buried four times. Ironically, almost two months to the day of his wife's death, Cariboo Cameron struck it rich. His gold find would be the second largest in the Cariboo, with his share coming close to $350,000. Another town, aptly named Cameron-town, would spring up in his honour.

Triumph and Tragedy

John Cameron

For a time, John Cameron would be one of the richest men in the Cariboo. But, unfortunately, his money didn't come in time to save his wife, Sophia, who died from typhoid fever (a.k.a. mountain fever) shortly before his first big gold strike. And Sophia Cameron was destined to be buried not once but four times.

The first time, just a few days after her death, John Cameron buried her in the Cariboo. As he watched the plain coffin sink into the autumn ground, he vowed once again to his dead wife that, eventually, she would be buried in her hometown of Cornwall, Ontario.

After striking it rich, Cameron lifted his wife's coffin from the cold Cariboo ground and prepared to take it to Victoria, the first step on the long journey back to Cornwall. Needing help with the transportation, he asked for volunteers. Even though he offered $12 a day and a bonus of $2,000, no one came forward. Finally, at the last minute, Cameron's partner, Robert Stevenson, offered to help. The two men spent 36 days travelling 400 miles in 40-below weather. They reached Victoria in early March, and Sophia Cameron was buried for the second time.

John Cameron returned to the Cariboo. The following November, however, he was back in Victoria. Sophia Cameron's grave was opened and the coffin was placed on a ship to Panama, destined for her beloved Cornwall. But even when Sophia Cameron's body arrived there, and was buried for a third time, it couldn't rest in peace — at least, not immediately. Someone started a rumour that the coffin didn't contain a body, but instead contained gold.

Cameron was devastated. He knew, however, that if he didn't do something to stop the rumours, the coffin would be vandalized and Sophia disturbed. So he invited a group of friends to the grave site, where the coffin was raised and opened and Sophia's body was displayed. Only then was his wife left to rest in peace.

Wanting to remain close to his beloved Sophia, John Cameron purchased a two hundred-acre farm in Cornwall and spent much of his fortune modernizing it. Unfortunately, that investment, along with several others, failed miserably. Cameron returned to Barkerville, naively thinking he could make another fortune. But mining had changed dramatically since he'd left, and Cameron was even lucky to find work as a labourer. Finally, on November 7, 1888, fifteen years to the day that Sophia Cameron's body had left Victoria, Cameron died. Friends of the broke and dispirited miner buried him near the old Cameron claim.

Sophia Cameron

News of the Barker and Cameron finds seemed to travel on the wind. Thousands and thousand of miners were bypassing the Fraser to get to the famous Williams Creek. They wanted to get in on the action, and as quickly as possible!

Travelling conditions around the Fraser River area had improved, but routes into the Cariboo were dangerous. One miner called British Columbia a "horse killing" country and said the animals were often "plunged up to the belly in swamps and mud."

Another prospector recalled his experience getting to Williams Creek. "Our track conducted us along the most frightful precipices. The rivers flow oftentimes through dark and awful gorges, whose rocky sides tower perpendicularly from a thousand to fifteen hundred feet. By a series of zigzag paths, often but a yard in width, man and beast have to traverse these scenes of grandeur. Sad and fatal accidents often occur, and horses and their owners are dashed to pieces on the rocks below, or drowned in the deep, foaming waters rushing down from mountain snow melting in the summer heat."

With all the gold being discovered in the Cariboo, James Douglas saw an opportunity. He wasn't after gold, but he did want a better transportation and communication system into the area. Barkerville was 600 miles from the Fraser River. Miners could take the Harrison-Lillooet Trail to get there, but the route wasn't ideal. They would have to travel at least partway on foot or by steamer, and anyone bringing in supplies had to transfer them back and forth several times from steamer to wagon. The route was clearly designed with the Fraser in mind. And with the exception of the Chinese miners, most men had left the Fraser. What the miners really needed was a road from Yale where supplies could be shipped directly to the Cariboo.

Death Strikes

Wooden stakes were posted randomly along the Cariboo route. Sometimes this was the only way men would learn about the death of friends. "We passed a stake on which was inscribed 'a young man is buried here; being killed by a bear at this spot.' Four or five miles further on we came upon another grave on which was written William S_____, aged 23. This saddened us, for we recognized the name as that of one of our fellow travellers from Panama, and a very pleasant companion we had found him."

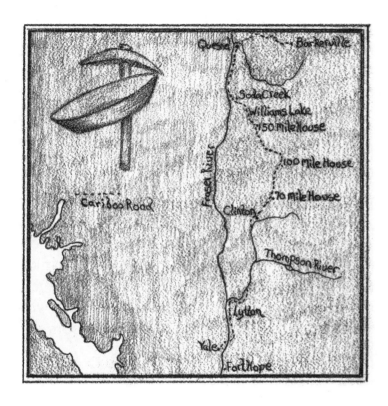

The Cariboo Road, which was used for twenty years until the arrival of the railroad, made travel to the gold fields much easier.

Douglas took a good look at the returns from the gold fields. They were high. Based on the promise of more gold, surely the newly established Bank of British Columbia would loan the province money to build a Cariboo Road. Douglas applied for the loan. Eventually it would come through, but he didn't bother waiting for an answer. In the spring of 1862, he put the first group of Royal Engineers to work. They built the first six-mile stretch. Under the most difficult conditions, through the toughest wilderness, men would continue to build the Cariboo Road for the next three years. It was eighteen feet wide and it was constructed almost entirely by hand — with picks and shovels and blasting powder. The road had to pass through walls of sheer rock. In other places, it spanned raging rivers on little more than giant cribs of logs. When it was finished in 1865, the Cariboo Road was four hundred miles long and was called the eighth wonder of the world. To help pay the $1 million price tag, Governor Douglas placed tolls on the road for seven years so future generations would be able to use it for free. Considered one of the finest roads in the world, it was Governor Douglas's greatest monument.

57

But by 1863, even before the road was finished, more and more people were travelling to the Cariboo. The gold takes were incredible. In 1863 alone, nearly $4 million in gold was lifted from the creeks and rivers of the B.C. interior. With that amount of gold at stake and a new road making travel easier, miners began to pour into the region.

They weren't alone. Like John Cameron before them, many of the men brought wives and families. Others weren't miners at all, but were judges, lawyers or business people of all description. They were the first settlers of B.C's Cariboo region, and they needed services like stores and banks, churches and schools. Soon the Cariboo communities began to grow. One of the most important communities of all was Barkerville. Eventually it would become the largest community west of Toronto and north of San Francisco.

Prices Fall

When construction began on the Cariboo Road, the price of buying supplies began to drop dramatically. In his book *Wagon Road North*, Art Downs says that in 1862 on Williams Creek, flour was $2 a pound, butter $5, nails $5 and potatoes $1.15 a pound. By 1864, even before the road was finished, flour had dropped to 35 cents a pound, butter $1.25 and potatoes 20 – 25 cents.

These men followed the footsteps of many who used a trundle-barrow or old-fashioned wheelbarrow to get supplies to the Cariboo.

Aside from Sophia Cameron, there weren't many women in the Cariboo when gold was first discovered. In fact, in 1862 there were between four thousand and six thousand people living in the area, yet only three or four of them were women.

Word soon travelled back to London, England, that there were large groups of unmarried miners in British Columbia's Cariboo. As a result, the British Columbia Emigration Society was formed to encourage respectable, industrious women to travel to the colony. The women were told they could find work as domestic servants, but the society really wanted them to marry the miners and establish a new colony in the Cariboo.

In the spring of 1862, sixty girls, many of them orphans, were put on a steamer called the *Tynemouth* to begin their trip to Esquimalt. Well-trained in the duties of domestic servants, the young girls were kept apart from the rest of the travellers and were heavily chaperoned by a matron and clergyman. While everyone else danced and partied, they could only watch and wonder what their future held.

If their time on board the *Tynemouth* was boring, their arrival at Victoria was not. As soon as word leaked out that the girls had arrived, men of all ages rushed to the docks to catch a glimpse of the "female cargo." The girls, who ranged in age from twelve to eighteen, marched two by two through the crowd of curious men. Thanks to the work of the Emigration Society, some of the girls already had jobs to go to; others married soon after their arrival.

Reaction to the undertaking was mixed; nevertheless, the society brought another group of thirty-six girls from England in early 1863. As soon as they arrived, twenty-five found jobs as servants.

The Journey of a Lifetime

William Hind joined the Overlanders and trekked across the prairies from Fort Garry to the Cariboo gold fields. His sketch shows the men travelling down the Fraser.

To travel to the Cariboo, most Easterners went by ship from New York to Panama, up to San Francisco and to Victoria. Some daring travellers, however, decided to go overland through the prairies and mountains to the gold fields. In 1862, a group from Ontario decided to do just that.

By today's standards, it doesn't sound like much of a trip. But back then, British Columbia was more remote from central Canada than even London or Paris. There were no roads. The mountains seemed impassable to traffic. Supplies were mainly obtained from Seattle and San Francisco.

The Overlanders gathered in spring at Fort Garry (near Winnipeg), where they bought horses, cattle and Red River carts to carry them as far as Edmonton. Beyond there, they were told, the cart trail didn't exist. They purchased flour and pemmican to eat. The flour was dark, heavy and wholesome; they paid $3.90 for 112 pounds of it. The pemmican, a mixture of pounded buffalo meat and grease formed into cakes, was six cents a pound.

With 150 people (including a woman and three young children), 110 animals and 97 carts marching through the wilderness, the group stretched across half a mile of land. Travel was extremely slow. They rose before dawn and split their day into two: travelling from 5 AM until noon, and again from 2 PM until six at night. They quickly decided they weren't getting far enough. They began travelling by 3 AM. Three hours later they'd stop for breakfast and a two-hour rest. Resuming at 8 AM, the day was again split into two shifts. This was far more efficient and allowed them to easily make their quota of twenty-five miles a day.

At night, the emigrants had to guard against native attack. Setting up camp, they placed their horses and cattle inside a triangle that they formed with their carts. Their tents were set up outside the triangle, and two watchmen stood guard through the night. Because of their caution, the group wasn't bothered by anyone.

The first few hundred miles took them along a well-marked and well-travelled route. After that, travelling conditions were sporadic. Some days the group made good time; other days they had to guess where the trail was taking them. Finally, on July 21, they popped out of the bush on the riverbanks opposite Edmonton, without even knowing how close they were to town. Exhausted, the group spent a week resting before resuming the final and most challenging leg of their journey.

Catherine Shubert was the only woman to travel with the Overlanders. She gave birth to a baby girl the day after she arrived at Kamloops.

Leaving a few people behind, 125 Overlanders began walking to the Cariboo. Instead of a winding trail of Red River carts, they had 150 pack animals loaded with 250 pounds of supplies, including 56 pounds of flour for each person. A few cattle were driven along for food. They travelled through swamps and streams, over hills and deep into forests. Sometimes the trails were so overgrown that men had to go ahead and chop out the brush and fallen timber. One traveller said: "A day's journey on the road to Jasper House generally consists of floundering through logs, varied by jumps and plunges over the timber which lies strewn, piled and interlaced along the path and on every side. The horses stick fast in the mire, tumble crashing amongst the logs, or driven to desperation, plunge amongst the thickly growing trees at the side."

A month out of Edmonton, the Overlanders were almost out of food. They had expected a two-month trip from Fort Garry and thought 168 pounds of flour and fifty pounds of pemmican per person would be enough. It wasn't. Almost three months had passed and they were just now on the shores of Cowdung Lake — the source of the Fraser. They were forced to use their guns and their wiles to obtain food. Dinner was often roasted skunk or porcupine, followed by wild huckleberries or perhaps wild saskatoons. Occasionally they'd meet friendly natives who would give them dried or fresh salmon.

They worried about food and worried about their route. They weren't sure how to get to the Cariboo. The native people they met couldn't help. Should they attempt to travel down the Fraser River to Quesnel, the Overlanders wondered, or should they continue overland to Kamloops? The group was split.

About twenty people, including the lone woman and her children, finally took the North Thompson River to Kamloops. The majority decided to try their luck on the raging Fraser.

They built rafts: large crude vessels lashed together with whatever they could find. The native people, amazed at the boldness of the travellers, shook their heads mournfully as raft after raft pushed off. The rafts drifted quickly with the river currents and soon reached the most dangerous part of the journey — the Grand Canyon. Some Overlanders were lucky. They made it through the treacherous waters safely. Others decided to travel by canoe. They weren't as lucky. The canoes were swamped in the water and a number of men drowned. Finally, on September 11, 1862, the first of the Overlanders arrived in Quesnel. They'd travelled over 3,500 miles in five months. Exhausted after their gruelling trip, many of them had no enthusiasm left for the rigors of the gold fields. Some became pioneer farmers in the B.C. interior, but the majority headed to the coast and settled in Victoria.

Chapter Six

BARKERVILLE & GOLD RUSH TIMES

Barkerville grew up right around the spot where Billy Barker found his gold. Soon to call itself the largest city west of Chicago and north of San Francisco, Barkerville would eventually have everything a person could need: laundries, blacksmiths, butchers, bakers, barbers, churches, a theatre, a newspaper, a cemetery, thirteen saloons, three breweries and even a sawmill.

In the beginning, however, the community was small and rough. The main street was narrow and muddy. Houses and stores were all built on stilts and all were at different heights. So were the sidewalks out front. Walking down the main street, people had to go from one level to the next every time they went from one building to another. The reason for the height: to protect houses and stores from the spring flooding that came from the creek. It was a true hodge-podge town with cattle wandering down the mud road and horses posted at random hitches every few feet.

But it wouldn't stay that way. By the time the Cariboo Road was almost finished, the standard of living was starting to improve in Barkerville. Rents there were the highest in the Cariboo. Even a portion of a house could command as much as $100 a month. Most miners, however, lived on the outskirts of town. Their quarters ranged from tents and dirt dugouts to lean-tos and sophisticated cabins.

As Fred Ludditt points out in his book

Barkerville the day before the famous fire.

Barkerville Days, even the most sophisticated cabins were built with simple axes, augers and, once in a while, a two-inch wood chisel. Nails were rarely used. Instead, logs to build the walls were "saddled" or cut to fit snugly together at the corners. At one end of every cabin was a fireplace. About four feet high and five feet wide, the fireplace was used for cooking and as a source of heat. Usually built with clay and boulders, it also provided light during dark winter nights. The roof of the cabin consisted of poles about five inches thick, and to keep out the cold, the small holes between the logs were generally stuffed with moss or clay.

Most miners didn't spend a whole lot of time alone in their cabins. They were either at work or at play. And play was usually done in the saloons.

Saloons were particularly important during gold rush times. They appeared all over the west: in tents, log cabins, even caves. Because a saloon was often one of the first buildings to go up in camp, it sometimes served as a town hall. Men would regularly go to saloons looking for work. Saloons also played a big role in the exchange of both news and rumours. In fact, it was in Bill McPhee's Saloon at Fortymile that George Washington Carmack would break the news of his gold find, starting off the Klondike stampede. But as well as serving as a place of business, saloons provided a welcome change from the hard work of mining. They served meals and liquor, had dance halls and even card rooms.

Barkerville saloons were proper wooden buildings, but some saloons were little more than tents.

Mixing Business and Pleasure

According to William Shannon, "crime in the far north was almost unknown. True, a great many of these men became addicted to liquor and gambling and came to an untimely end in this way, but can this be wondered at when we consider the circumstances that surrounded them, secluded in the mountains and cut off from their family circle and the beneficial influences of Christianity? Man is a social being, and in this way they often become addicted to drink."

The saloon in the mining camp was the post office and business place, as well as the place where the miners congregated to have a social time and tell each other their experiences. After hitting pay dirt, most miners would head for the saloons. One fellow, who took out forty thousand dollars in gold nuggets, went to the best saloon in Barkerville, where he called in guests from the street and treated them to champagne that cost more than thirty dollars a bottle. When his "guests" couldn't drink any more, he ordered every glass in the house filled and placed on the bar. With one sweep of his hand, he sent the glasses smashing to the floor. But there was still a basket of champagne left. He danced on it until he cut his feet. He still wasn't satisfied.

After all, he had some gold nuggets left. Looking around the saloon, he spotted a mirror worth hundreds of dollars hanging on the wall. Gathering his last nuggets, he hurled them in handfuls at the glass. Only then did he stagger out into the night, where he slept under the stars, as broke as he had been before he discovered his nuggets earlier that day.

Scotty's Ranch was a popular Cariboo saloon where miners could get drinks like "cobblers" or "streaks of lightning." Most of the available whiskey wasn't especially smooth; it was known to make even the most seasoned drinker's throat raw. Most of the time miners were encouraged to help themselves by pouring from the "spirit-bottle" at the bar. It was a common (and expensive) habit for miners to "treat" their friends. "A member of our party allowed himself to be persuaded into accepting two such free drinks from a miner who entered the tavern with fifty-two dollars of hard-earned money, all of which he spent in drinking here, and treating the company present. Our friend was rendered unfit for travel for days, through the two draughts of the mixture. It completely upset him and much rest, fresh air and exercise were needed to restore him to his previous vigorous health."

Communicating

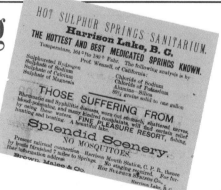

The *Cariboo Sentinel* was the first newspaper to be published in the Barkerville area. The first issue came out June 6, 1865. Operating for ten years, the weekly was full of advertising, editorials, community notices and letters. An early issue contained a letter to the editor written by the local Barkerville doctor. It highlights the health concerns facing the Barkerville pioneers.

Sir:

In the summer of 1863, there were typhoid symptoms which proved fatal to some. During the past season frost bites and scurvy have entirely vanished. Better cabins and a plentiful supply of vegetables have caused this. The cold, though intense, was unaccompanied by the piercing wind so frequent in other countries. During the winter months only three patients were admitted to the hospital. One had diseased lungs, another was a case of rheumatism and the third an accident. The general health of the creek is good and I've no doubt that a moderately warm season and plenty of "dust" will keep both body and mind healthy.

I am,
Yours obediently,
John Chipps, Physician at
W.C. (Williams Creek) Hospital

Good Health Does Grow On Trees

One old prospector by the name of Fauquier Mac-Lennan didn't bother with hospital remedies. And he became something of a local hero when he saved the lives of a number of miners suffering from scurvy. At first the men thought they had rheumatism. But Mac-Lennan, who was in the Cariboo from his home way up north, said it was scurvy. And, he told the men, the cure was right outside their cabin door.

He told them to boil the boughs of the spruce tree and drink at least a dozen cups of the brew every day. They did, and without spending a single penny on medicine, the men were well enough to go back to work in four days.

The doctor's office and log hospital were simple affairs.

Some miners, like Ned Stout, wouldn't touch a drop of alcohol. Years later they would say that's why they lived such long lives. Whether it was true or not, many Cariboo residents died young, as the cemetery at Barkerville shows. It wasn't unusual for men and women to die in their twenties or early thirties. People rarely lived beyond the age of forty-five. Cause of death varied. There were accidents like avalanches and snowstorms, but there were also causes of death that occurred over and over again. Some miners fell down mine shafts. Others worked long hours in freezing water and died from rheumatism. Still others, like John Cameron's wife, Sophia, died from mountain fever.

The miners were aware of the medical risks they faced. They'd watched John Cameron's wife die. And she wasn't the only one to die of typhoid fever in those early months at Barkerville. So, in the spring of 1863, a group of miners petitioned the government for a hospital. They presented their demands to Judge Begbie. A small amount of government money was put forward, but it wasn't enough. Most of the money was raised by the miners themselves. And in late August, the log hospital building was started. When it officially opened in October, it consisted of one ward, a doctor's office and a kitchen. By then the population of Williams Creek, or Barkerville, had climbed to 6,000 people. About 4,000 of them were miners.

The Cariboo Camels

For a time, camels were used to carry supplies in the Cariboo.

Frank Laumeister figured if there was good money in packing freight into the camps, he could make even more money by finding animals that could carry heavier loads.

One animal that was sure-footed (a must for the treacherous Cariboo trails) and could also carry up to 800 pounds on its back was the camel.

In 1862, Laumeister bought twenty-three camels from the U.S. army. He paid $300 for each of them, a small fortune in those days. They came up the Fraser by boat and as they were unloaded at Port Douglas, store-keepers and bystanders stared at the humpbacked animals in disbelief.

The camels quickly adapted to the Canadian climate. Just as quickly, they put the mules to shame. As well as carrying the expected 800 pounds, they could travel thirty-five miles a day.

But there were problems. For one thing, their hooves were designed for sand, not rock. When some of the animals went lame, Laumeister fitted them with rawhide boots. That helped. But he couldn't do anything about the way the animals smelled.

And they smelled terrible — especially to the packhorses and mules. Everywhere the camels went, the mules and horses bolted. Valuables were strewn all over the trails. Laumeister dosed the camels with perfumed water. It didn't help. Worst of all, other drivers began suing Laumeister.

In the end, Laumeister turned the camels loose on the Thompson River flats. Some died from the bitter winter cold. Others spent years wandering in the wilderness.

With more people in the area, more supplies were needed. Some of the hardest workers weren't the miners at all, but the people who delivered food, equipment and other necessities to Barkerville and the nearby camps. With the opening of the Cariboo Road, there were more options for drivers. Mules and pony expresses began to appear. A good mule could cover the distance from Yale to Quesnel in a month, leaping casually through the treacherous Fraser Canyon carrying a 250-pound load. At $1.00 a pound, most mule trains made good money.

The mule trains were usually made up of sixteen to fifty animals. No pack saddles were used. Instead, a rough leather sack filled with straw and called an "aparajoe" was girded tightly to the mule's back. A strong hitch was used to lash the freight, which could weigh up to four hundred pounds. Leading the train was a bell animal, usually a white mare.

Packhorses were also popular. The packhorse was a hardy, half-wild pony sometimes called a bronco. Intelligent, sure-footed and usually able to forage for itself, it could carry from 150 to 250 pounds. In the southern interior, they could be purchased off the range for $5 to $10 each. When "broken" or saddle trained, they could run as high as $50 or more.

Packing the horses or mules with baggage required great skill. Most miners hired someone to do the job for them. They were called packers, and they could earn up to thirty cents per pound of baggage. Experienced packers were sought after, and many travelled alongside the miners in order to reload the horses or mules when it was necessary. Most animals became upset when loaded with baggage, but in the hands of a good packer they quickly settled down.

Mail Delivery

By the time Barkerville was established, so was regular mail service between Victoria and points northward. Prior to that, however, mail delivery relied first on distribution by the Hudson's Bay Company and then on the kindness of officials from the various steamships. Sometimes they would charge up to $5 to deliver just one letter.

By 1861, however, a man named Frances Jones Barnard began running a much-needed express service. He wasn't the first man to run an express. As early as 1858, Billy Ballou had carried mail, parcels and newspapers to the mining camps.

But Barnard stood out from the crowd. A Frenchman from Quebec City, he was rugged, dependable and strong. At first he carried letters and papers by foot from Yale to the Cariboo and back again—a distance of 760 miles. The following year, after a particularly wicked winter, he established a pony express from Yale to Barkerville. So did Billy Ballou. But competition between the two men was about to come to an end.

Governor Douglas wanted to streamline the mail service. The colonies had their own stamps now—they'd had them since 1861. They were pink and bore a profile view of Queen Victoria. Rather than have a number of different people responsible for mail distribution into the camps and mining communities, Douglas wanted one person to do it all. Ballou and Barnard both bid for the job. Barnard won.

Within a year, Barnard developed his pony express into a two-horse wagon, running every ten days and carrying two or three passengers. During the winter of 1863-64, sleighs were used in place of wagons to keep connections open with the Cariboo. By 1864, Barnard had fourteen-passenger four-horse stages on the road from Yale to Soda Creek, carrying mail, express and passengers. Above Quesnel, a saddle train connected with the stages until the completion of the road in 1865. And to satisfy fears of highway robbery, he outfitted his wagons with iron, burglar-proof safes.

Stagecoaches also began to travel the Cariboo Road into Barkerville, bringing mail, supplies and a variety of passengers, including dance hall girls.

Even though the miners found time to go dancing, most of their hours were devoted to mining. If the Fraser had challenged the men, the Cariboo challenged them more. And if their own efforts didn't pay off, they probably knew someone who had struck it rich. In 1863, the most productive year for placer gold in B.C.'s history, it seemed the harvest of gold from Williams Creek was never-ending. One claim, the Cunningham, produced roughly $2,000 every day during the mining season.

Actually, the yields from Williams Creek stayed well above $3,000,000 for the next two years. Some records suggest the yields were closer to $6,000,000 each year—much of it hidden or undeclared.

Of course, much of that money was spent in saloons—those gathering places where business so easily mixed with pleasure. And it was an incident in Barry and Adler's saloon that would change the course of Barkerville's history forever.

No one is sure exactly what happened, but on September 16, 1868, in a little over an hour, Barkerville burned to the ground. Some say the fire was caused by a miner knocking over a lamp; others insist it was a hot iron that started it. Most believe the blaze began when a miner tried to steal a kiss from a dance hall girl. He bumped into a stove and knocked a pipe from the canvas ceiling.

Whatever its cause, the fire spread rapidly. Photographer Frederick Dally saw the fire. He said: "The fire travelled up and down both sides of the street—and although my building was nearly fifty yards away from where the fire originated, in less than twenty minutes it, together with the whole lower part of the town, was a sheet of fire, hissing, crackling and roaring furiously. There was, in a store not far from my place, fifty kegs of blasting powder and had that not been removed at the commencement of the fire, and put down a dry shaft, most likely not a soul would have been left alive. Blankets and bedding were sent at least 200 feet high when a number of coal oil tins, five gallons, exploded."

Rebuilding started immediately. The *Cariboo Sentinel* reported seven days after the fire: "Already there are over thirty houses standing in symmetrical order on the old site, and the foundation of several others laid…The town, when rebuilt will present a much more uniform and pleasant appearance."

It was true enough. Barkerville was almost completely rebuilt a year later, and most people thought it was more attractive than ever. But the fire, coupled with new directions in mining, changed things in Barkerville forever. The Cariboo gold rush was over. In years to come, Barkerville would become one of British Columbia's most famous ghost towns.

Chapter Seven

THE MINERS MOVE ON

The Davis claim on Williams Creek, where the Cornish wheel was used to keep the mine shaft dry.

Miners in the Cariboo were getting tired. Placer diggings along the creeks were drying up. Some men had moved to the nearby mountains where there was more gold, but conditions there were worse. They had to dig—and dig hard. It was called "wet sinking," or driving shafts into the ground. Around the clock they worked, and often they would find themselves up to their knees in water and silt—a mixture they called Cariboo slum.

As well as enduring tough physical conditions, the miners watched with dismay as big businesses began to take over. Picks, shovels and pans were replaced by much more sophisticated—and expensive—methods. Only the wealthy could afford to build sluices and flumes, giant wheels and pumps. Claim after claim was sold to large mining companies. Some of those companies ended up broke when the Cariboo slum destroyed their equipment. Those that did stay employed many men, but the wages were barely enough for the miners to survive on.

Even the bigger companies were forced to change some of their ways. When underground mining became too expensive, they blasted the creeks and ravines with high-powered streams of water. The wet sludge was put through a whole series of sluices in order to capture every last bit of gold. By the early 1870s, there were five steam engines, 27 waterwheels, 13 tunnels, 63 shafts, 43 hydraulics and 23 ground sluices in the Cariboo.

Gold still continued to leave the Williams Creek area. In fact, total output from that creek and two of its tributaries, Conklin and Stout's Gulch, was estimated to be between $30 million and $40 million from 1861 to 1898.

69

Tragedy at Sea

As the gold rush ended, some miners decided to take whatever riches they had accumulated and go back home. To the joy of the families waiting for them, most made it home safely. A few, however, did not.

One of the biggest tragedies to occur as the gold rush waned was the sinking of the sidewheeler *Pacific*. Hundreds of lives were lost, and the gold and silver that sank during the accident remains at the bottom of the ocean today.

The *Pacific* had travelled the Fraser River during the gold rush of 1858, but by 1872 officials had decided the old boat wasn't very seaworthy. When miners began discovering gold in the Kootenay and Omineca regions, however, and travel between Victoria and California picked up again, officials decided to put the boat back to work.

The *Pacific* steamed out of Victoria harbour November 4, 1875. On board were hundreds of people; many of them were miners loaded with gold and heading for San Francisco. Impatient to get home, some of the miners didn't bother buying tickets. They simply walked onto an already overloaded ship.

Heading below deck, the miners joined some of the other businessmen in a few rounds of gambling. The first part of the trip was uneventful. But unfortunately, as the *Pacific* emerged from the Strait of Juan de Fuca and rounded Cape Flattery, she was struck by the *Orpheus*, a sailing ship travelling to B.C. for coal. Damage was so extensive that the *Pacific* began to sink almost immediately. There wasn't even time to launch the lifeboats. Quickly she sank, drowning all but two passengers and taking down cargo valued at $100,000. (Today that silver and gold, which still lies off Cape Flattery, would be worth more than one million dollars.)

Hundreds of lives and thousands of dollars in gold and silver were lost when the *Pacific* sank in 1875.

Slowly, surface mining declined. Giant companies like Hobson's Bullion Mine near Likely and Ward's Mine on the Horsefly took over. Many miners gave up. Some, broke and discouraged, returned home to England or eastern Canada. Others stayed and built a life in either the Cariboo or near the Fraser — a life that revolved around ranching or selling rather than prospecting. There were others, however, who weren't prepared to give up. Gold was what brought them to British Columbia and gold would keep them there.

Their attention was captured by the East Kootenays, where an earlier find on the rough Wild Horse Creek was beginning to pay off. There was also a flurry of activity on the "Big Bend" of the Columbia River, north of the current city of Revelstoke. Men began to stake claims near the head of the Columbia and in other parts of the Kootenays. In the early 1870s, prospecting also went on near the headwaters of the Omineca, and while miners attempted to keep quiet about the gold and silver being found in the rivers and streams there, eventually word got out and another small rush was underway. Moderate amounts of gold were found on Big Bend, and the Omineca yielded well for a few

GHOST TOWNS

Many of the booming gold camps of years ago have vanished. For instance, one of the first communities to appear on Williams Creek was Richfield, described in 1863 by a journalist as "comprising the ordinary series of rough wooden shanties, stores, restaurants, grog shops, and gambling saloons." But a few years later, when the gold dried up, the community became deserted. Soon it had virtually disappeared. The same thing happened to the communities of Van Winkle and Antler Creek.

Barkerville, however, died and was reborn. The town that burned to the ground in 1868 never did regain its former glory. As the miners moved on, the town became less populated. Although called a ghost town by many, in actual fact roughly fifty people have always lived in or around Barkerville.

In 1959, Barkerville was declared a Provincial Historic Park. Restoration work has been ongoing ever since. Today there are over 80 original buildings and over 110 display areas. And on Highway 26, between Barkerville and Quesnel, is one of the last remaining roadhouses on the old Cariboo Highway, Cottonwood House.

Other communities that grew up because of the gold rush flourished. Quesnel is a good example. In the early 1860s, Quesnel was the gateway to Barkerville. Today it's home to 8,000 people. Many of them take part in "Billy Barker Days," a gold rush celebration held each July.

The town of Richfield as it was in 1863.

Gold Panning Today

Serious miners must buy a free miner's certificate and must also "stake a claim." A claim must be registered with the gold commissioner's office, and once that claim is registered, a certain amount of work must be done every year in order for the claim to remain active. If work stops, the claim comes open and can be staked and utilized by someone else.

People interested in hand panning on a recreational or casual basis don't need to buy a free miner's certificate. In the Princeton area, officials at the tourist bureau will rent you a gold pan and show you a map outlining spots where you can hand pan for gold.

Those who want to search for gold today must do their digging in designated areas. The Ministry of Energy, Mines and Petroleum Resources has designated fifteen percent of British Columbia open to placer mining. These are areas where gold is most likely to be found.

You do need permission to hand pan in an area that has already been claimed. To get this, contact the B.C. Mining Association or the individual claim holder.

years, but neither area produced anything close to the riches of the Cariboo.

By the time Barkerville had burned and been rebuilt, the Cariboo gold rush had peaked and dropped. But the province that had once been known as New Caledonia had changed forever.

An economic depression was sweeping through Vancouver Island and other parts of British Columbia. Men and women were restless and dissatisfied. They wanted solutions to their money problems. They looked to the local government and weren't happy with what they saw. They wanted a more mature form of government. Some suggested the colony should move away from its British connection and join with the United States. Others disagreed. They looked to eastern Canada — over the route taken not so many years before by the Overlanders. There was potential for help there, but they needed a link between

Resolving Disputes

Currently, there are seven mining divisions in the province of British Columbia. Each mining division is administered by a gold commissioner. The gold commissioners are responsible for registering all claims and for resolving disputes between miners and private land owners. The chief gold commissioner of British Columbia also presides over "miners' court." If one person accuses another of not staking a claim properly or of not keeping a claim active, the chief gold commissioner will investigate and make a decision.

Today most claim disputes are resolved in the gold commissioner's office, but during gold rush times, miners (seen here guarding a claim) would often take the law into their own hands.

east and west — a physical link much like the Cariboo Road that had linked Barkerville with the lower Fraser.

On September 14, 1868, just two days before the infamous Barkerville fire, the Yale Convention was held. Twenty-six men decided that immediate union with Canada was the ideal. It wouldn't happen right away, but in 1871 British Columbia became a Canadian province.

The gold rush had come and the gold rush had gone. But because of it, the province of British Columbia had changed forever. There were roads and waterways connecting the capital of Victoria to places like Fort Hope, Fort Yale and Barkerville. There was mail service now and, thanks to the early efforts of Judge Begbie, a strong police force. There were towns and settlements springing out of the wilderness.

Riches From The Ranch

The Cornwall Ranch in the Thompson-Nicola valley was just one of many settlements that sprang up during the gold rush.

Some men discovered riches away from the gold fields. American Robert Carson was one of those men. Lured to British Columbia by the thought of gold, he made his way up the Fraser Canyon, eventually working with his own pack train. But it wasn't packing supplies to the camps that would make him rich. It was growing them.

While travelling south of the Cariboo, Carson discovered the summit of Pavilion Mountain. As his horses grazed on the wild grass that grew in the surrounding pastures, Carson had time to dream. And in his dreams he saw the potential for a ranch. It didn't matter that the area was isolated or that there would be few people around to buy what he grew; he decided to settle there.

He went to work chopping trees, digging irrigation ditches and building a house, barn and fences for livestock. His work didn't go unnoticed. A traveller passing through the

the area in 1860 noted, "In Pavilion Valley excellent crops of cereals and vegetables are produced. The crop of potatoes reaped by the proprietor of a farm at Pavilion gave 325 bushels to the acre. One of the turnips grown in his garden weighed 26 pounds. Oats and barley thrived under this gentleman's care. His cattle were allowed to run at large without shelter during the winter, gathering provisions as best they could."

By the time the Cariboo gold rush was underway, Carson realized people weren't going to come to him — he had to go to them. He began selling pork and produce in Clinton. He drove cattle along the Harrison route to Lillooet Lake and Vancouver. Eventually, the Carson ranch would become a provincial landmark. Many, many people enjoyed its hospitality as they travelled by horseback or stagecoach up the Fraser to the Cariboo.

The lower Fraser River, once home to miners with picks and shovels and pans, was now surrounded by a thriving farming community. Wheat was being grown; cattle were being raised. Barrel makers and blacksmiths were setting up shop. West of the farms were Burrard Inlet and the town of "Granville," destined one day to become the city of Vancouver. In spite of the depression and the end of the gold rush, people were excited about the future. About the possibility of joining with Canada. About the coming of the railroad.

According to John Tod, "all along the banks of the Fraser may be seen, in striking contrast to that of former times, thriving little villages, well stocked farms, tastefully ornamented cottages, inhabited generally by a young and hardy race."

Many of the men and women living on those farms had been lured away from comfortable homes to search for one thing: gold. And in the process they brought civilization to one corner of the world. They brought civilization to British Columbia.

Clearing the land at Granville circa 1885.

B.C. Mining Today

Mining continues to be important to the economy of British Columbia. It is this province's second largest industry and generates $2.3 billion every year. There are several large mining operations in B.C.; most emphasize mining for copper, lead or zinc.

The biggest producing gold mine in British Columbia was the Bralorne/Pioneer mine. It was worked from 1932 to 1971 and produced 4.1 million ounces of gold. Bralorne was the sixth largest producer in Canada.

Placer mining still goes on in British Columbia. Most summers there are about fifty operations underway ranging from individuals to small companies with a few employees. Most of the work is centred in the Cariboo—around the Barkerville/Wells area, although some also takes place in the Omineca and Kootenay regions.

The finds, however, are much smaller than they used to be. Ten dollars of gold taken from a cubic metre of gravel is considered a good gold find.

Glossary

alchemy: a mixture of science, magic and religion used in the Middle Ages to turn base metals into gold and to find an elixir of life. It eventually turned into the study of chemistry.

alloy: a mixture of two or more metals, or of a metal and another substance

alluvium: particles of rock transported and deposited by rivers

auger: a tool for drilling holes into wood or the ground bar gravel stretching into a creek or river

bar diggings: a mine between the high- and low-water marks on a river, lake or other body of water

base metal: any of the common, nonprecious metals

bedrock: solid rock beneath loose surface of the ground

black sand: mixture of heavy dark minerals and metals

bonanza: rich find of precious metals

bunkhouse: a small cabin with beds

Cariboo slum: a mixture of water and silt

claim: parcel of land legally held for mining purposes

colours: small particles of visible gold

cradle: *see rocker*

creek diggings: a mine in the bed of a stream or ravine

diggings: location of mining activity

ditch: a narrow, shallow trench

dredging: raising gold-bearing gravel from rivers or creeks

dry diggings: a mine where water has not flowed

el dorado: a Spanish term meaning "the golden place"

factor: the local boss of the Hudson's Bay Co.

flume: a sloped ditch used to convey water

flour gold: gold dust

fool's gold: iron pyrite sometimes mistaken for gold

freshet: a rush of fresh water

hardtack: flour and water mixed, baked and used as a bread substitute

Hudson's Bay Company: an English company that controlled the fur trade in New Caledonia

hydraulic: water pressure used to cut away banks or gravel

lode gold: a vein or pocket of gold running through a rock

motherlode: the original starting place or source of gold

mountain fever: typhoid fever

mule train: a group of mules used to transport goods

nugget: a lump of gold valued at $1 or more

ore: rock containing profitable amounts of metal

packer: men experienced in packing horses and mules

packhorse: a horse used to transport goods

panning: removing gold particles from the soil or gravel by washing it in a pan

pay dirt: rich, gold-containing placer findings

placer creek: a creek containing loose or free gold

placer gold: loose or free gold deposited in soil or gravel

poke: a small leather bag miners used for storing and carrying gold

potlatch: a native community celebration that includes feasting and gift-giving

precious stone: a deposit of precious stones in veins, beds or diggings

prospectors: people who explore for something, often gold

provisions: food supplies

quartz: rock made of silica and oxygen, often gold-bearing

riffle: a ledge or apron-like device in the bottom of a rocker that catches gold as it is washed

rocker: portable sluice that rocks for gold washing

shaft: a mine hole dug to gain access to gold

shafthouse: the structure housing equipment at the top of the mine

shanty: a rough cabin, often where prospectors lived

sidewheeler: a paddle-wheel-driven boat with wheels on each side

sluice: riffled trough for washing placer gold ore, bigger than a rocker

stake: to legally claim ground

sternwheeler: a paddle-wheel-driven boat with one large wheel at the stern or back end

stream deposits: deposits formed by running water

tailings: the discarded rocks that are separated out or removed to recover gold lying on the bedrock

vein: a thin line of gold usually found in rock seams

waterwheel: a wheel rotated by water

wet sinking: a Cariboo term for driving shafts into the ground

Bibliography

Akrigg, G.P.V. and Akrigg, Helen. *B.C Chronicle 1847 – Gold and the Colonists*. Discovery Press, Vancouver, 1977.

Barlee, N.L. *The Guide to Gold Panning in British Columbia*. Canada West Publications, 1979.

Barlee, N.L. *Historic Treasures and Lost Mines*. Hancock House, 1993.

Beeson, Edith. *Dunlevy – From the Diaries of Alex P. McInnes*. Lillooet Publishing, 1971.

Cohen, Daniel. *Gold: The Fascinating Story of the Noble Metal Through the Ages*. M. Evans, New York, 1976.

Downs, Art. *Wagon Road North*. Heritage House Publishing, revised 1993.

Elliott, Gordon. *Barkerville, Quesnel and the Cariboo Gold Rush*. Douglas & McIntyre Ltd., Vancouver, 1980.

Hill, Beth. *Sappers: The Royal Engineers in British Columbia*. Horsdal and Schubart, Ganges, 1987.

Ludditt, Fred. *Barkerville Days*. Mr. Paperback, Langley, 1969.

Neering, Rosemary. *Gold Rush*. Fitzhenry and Whiteside, 1984.

Ormsby, Margaret. *British Columbia, A History*. Macmillan, 1958/64.

Pioneer Days of British Columbia. Volumes One, Two and Three.

Place, Marian T. *Cariboo Gold*. Holt, Rinehart and Winston. 1970.

Vallance, J.D. *Untrodden Ways*. Hebden Printing, 1975.

Waite, Donald E. *The Cariboo Gold Rush*. Hancock House Publishers, 1988.

Index